Simple 1-2-3™
Cooking for Kids

Publications International, Ltd.

Favorite Brand Name Recipes at www.fbnr.com

Photography on pages 5, 7, 10, 16, 19, 27, 59, 81, 87 and 104 by Proffitt Photography Ltd.
Photographer: Laurie Proffitt
Photographer's Assistant: Chad Evans
Food Stylist: Becky Roller
Assistant Food Stylist: Nora Alfonsi

Ingredient photography by Shaughnessy MacDonald, Inc.

Pictured on the front cover: Octo-Dog and Shells *(page 83)*.

Pictured on the back cover *(clockwise from top left):* Tuna Schooners *(page 59),* Mini Turtle Cupcakes *(page 129)* and Monster Mouth *(page 85)*.

ISBN-13: 978-1-4127-2175-2
ISBN-10: 1-4127-2175-X

Library of Congress Control Number: 2004115113

Manufactured in China.

8 7 6 5 4 3 2 1

Microwave Cooking: Microwave ovens vary in wattage. Use the cooking times as guidelines and check for doneness before adding more time.

Preparation/Cooking Times: Preparation times are based on the approximate amount of time required to assemble the recipe before cooking, baking, chilling or serving. These times include preparation steps such as measuring, chopping and mixing. The fact that some preparations and cooking can be done simultaneously is taken into account. Preparation of optional ingredients and serving suggestions is not included.

Contents

Rise & Shine

French Toast Sticks

1 cup EGG BEATERS®
⅓ cup skim milk
1 teaspoon ground cinnamon
1 teaspoon vanilla extract
2 tablespoons FLEISCHMANN'S® Original Margarine, divided
16 (4×1×1-inch) sticks day-old white bread
Powdered sugar (optional)
Maple-flavored syrup (optional)

1. In shallow bowl, combine Egg Beaters®, milk, cinnamon and vanilla.

2. In large nonstick griddle or skillet, over medium-high heat, melt 2 teaspoons margarine. Dip bread sticks in egg mixture to coat; transfer to griddle. Cook sticks on each side until golden, adding remaining margarine as needed.

3. Dust lightly with powdered sugar and serve with syrup, if desired.

Makes 4 servings

Prep Time: *15 minutes*
Cook Time: *18 minutes*

2½ cups all-purpose flour
¾ cup packed brown sugar
¾ cup chopped dried apples
½ cup golden raisins
2 teaspoons baking powder
1¼ teaspoons ground cinnamon
½ teaspoon baking soda
¼ teaspoon salt
2 eggs
1½ cups milk
¼ cup vegetable oil
1 teaspoon butter
Maple-flavored syrup (optional)

Apple Orchard Pancakes

1. Combine flour, brown sugar, apples, raisins, baking powder, cinnamon, baking soda and salt in large bowl; mix well.

2. Beat eggs in medium bowl; stir in milk and oil. Add to flour mixture; stir just until blended.

3. Lightly coat griddle with butter. Heat over medium heat until hot. Pour about ¼ cup batter onto griddle for each pancake. Cook until bubbles form and bottom of pancakes are golden brown; turn and cook about 2 minutes or until brown and cooked through. Repeat with remaining batter. Serve pancakes with syrup, if desired. *Makes about 20 pancakes*

Strawberry Muffins

1. Preheat oven to 425°F. Grease bottoms only of 12 (2½-inch) muffin cups or line with paper liners; set aside.

2. Combine flour, baking powder and salt in large bowl. Stir in oats and sugar. Combine milk, butter, egg and vanilla in small bowl until well blended; stir into flour mixture just until moistened. Fold in strawberries. Spoon into prepared muffin cups, filling about two-thirds full.

3. Bake 15 to 18 minutes or until lightly browned and toothpick inserted in centers comes out clean. Remove from pan. Cool on wire rack 10 minutes. Serve warm or cool completely.

Makes 12 muffins

1¼ cups all-purpose flour
2½ teaspoons baking powder
½ teaspoon salt
1 cup uncooked old-fashioned oats
½ cup sugar
1 cup milk
½ cup butter, melted
1 egg, beaten
1 teaspoon vanilla
1 cup chopped fresh strawberries

Wafflewich

2 frozen cinnamon waffles
25 miniature marshmallows
2 tablespoons JIF® Creamy
   Peanut Butter
½ banana, sliced
¼ cup chocolate chips

1. Toast waffles until desired doneness.

2. Heat marshmallows and peanut butter in microwave until melted; stir until blended and smooth. Spread mixture on 1 waffle.

3. Arrange banana slices over peanut butter mixture; top with chocolate chips and remaining waffle.   *Makes 1 wafflewich*

Triple Berry Breakfast Parfait

1. Combine yogurt and cinnamon in small bowl.

2. Combine strawberries, blueberries and raspberries in medium bowl.

3. For each parfait, layer ¼ cup fruit mixture, 2 tablespoons granola and ¼ cup yogurt mixture in parfait glass. Repeat layers. Garnish with mint leaves, if desired.

Makes 4 servings

2 cups vanilla-flavored yogurt
¼ teaspoon ground cinnamon
1 cup sliced strawberries
½ cup blueberries
½ cup raspberries
1 cup low-fat granola without raisins

2 turkey breakfast sausage
  patties
3 eggs
  Salt and pepper
2 teaspoons butter
2 slices Cheddar cheese
2 whole wheat English
  muffins, split and
  toasted

Quick Breakfast Sandwich

1. Cook sausage according to package directions; set aside and keep warm.

2. Beat eggs in small bowl with salt and pepper to taste. Melt butter in small skillet. Pour in eggs; cook and stir gently over low heat until just set.

3. Place cheese on bottom halves of English muffins; top with sausage, scrambled eggs and muffin tops. Serve immediately.   *Makes 2 sandwiches*

Tip: Turkey breakfast sausage patties may vary in size. If patties are small, use two patties for each sandwich.

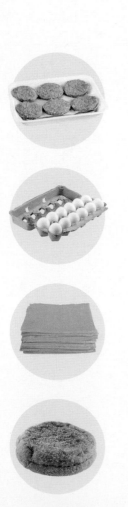

French Raisin Toast

1. Combine granulated sugar and cinnamon in wide shallow bowl. Beat in eggs and milk. Add bread; let stand to coat, then turn to coat other side.

2. Heat 2 tablespoons butter in large skillet over medium-low heat. Add 4 bread slices; cook until brown. Turn and cook other side. Remove and keep warm. Repeat with remaining butter and bread.

3. Sprinkle with powdered sugar; garnish as desired. Serve immediately.

Makes 4 servings

2 tablespoons granulated sugar
1 teaspoon ground cinnamon
4 eggs, lightly beaten
½ cup milk
8 slices raisin bread
4 tablespoons butter or margarine, divided
Powdered sugar

Toll House® Mini Morsel Pancakes

2½ cups all-purpose flour
1 cup (6 ounces) NESTLÉ®
   TOLL HOUSE®
   Semi-Sweet Chocolate
   Mini Morsels
1 tablespoon baking
   powder
½ teaspoon salt
1¾ cups milk
2 large eggs
⅓ cup vegetable oil
⅓ cup packed brown sugar
   Powdered sugar
   Fresh sliced strawberries
   Maple syrup

COMBINE flour, morsels, baking powder and salt in large bowl. Combine milk, eggs, vegetable oil and brown sugar in medium bowl; add to flour mixture. Stir just until moistened (batter may be lumpy).

HEAT griddle or skillet over medium heat; brush lightly with vegetable oil. Pour ¼ *cup* of batter onto hot griddle; cook until bubbles begin to burst. Turn; continue to cook for about 1 minute longer or until golden. Repeat with *remaining* batter.

SPRINKLE with powdered sugar; top with strawberries. Serve with maple syrup.

Makes about 18 pancakes

Berry Filled Muffins

1. Preheat oven to 400°F. Place 8 (2½-inch) paper or foil liners in muffin cups; set aside. Rinse blueberries from Mix with cold water and drain.

2. Empty muffin mix into bowl. Break up any lumps. Add egg and water. Stir until moistened, about 50 strokes. Fill cups half full with batter.

3. Fold blueberries into jam. Spoon on top of batter in each cup. Spread gently. Cover with remaining batter. Sprinkle with almonds. Bake at 400°F for 17 to 20 minutes or until set and golden brown. Cool in pan 5 to 10 minutes. Loosen carefully before removing from pan.   *Makes 8 muffins*

Tip: For a delicious flavor variation, try using blackberry or red raspberry jam instead of the strawberry jam.

1 package DUNCAN HINES® Bakery-Style Wild Maine Blueberry Muffin Mix
1 egg
½ cup water
¼ cup strawberry jam
2 tablespoons sliced natural almonds

Breakfast Pizza

1 can (10 ounces)
   refrigerated biscuit
   dough
½ pound bacon slices
2 tablespoons butter or
   margarine
2 tablespoons all-purpose
   flour
¼ teaspoon salt
⅛ teaspoon black pepper
1½ cups milk
½ cup (2 ounces) shredded
   sharp Cheddar cheese
¼ cup sliced green onions
¼ cup chopped red bell
   pepper

1. Preheat oven to 350°F. Spray 13×9-inch baking dish with nonstick cooking spray. Separate biscuit dough and arrange in rectangle on lightly floured surface. Roll into 14×10-inch rectangle. Place in prepared dish; pat edges up sides of dish. Bake 15 minutes. Remove from oven and set aside.

2. Meanwhile, place bacon in single layer in large skillet; cook over medium heat until crisp. Remove from skillet; drain on paper towels. Crumble and set aside.

3. Melt butter in medium saucepan over medium heat. Stir in flour, salt and black pepper until smooth. Gradually stir in milk; cook and stir until thickened. Stir in cheese until melted. Spread sauce evenly over baked crust. Sprinkle bacon, green onions and bell pepper over sauce. Bake, uncovered, 20 minutes or until crust is golden brown. Cut into 6 wedges. *Makes 6 servings*

Banana Bread Waffles with Cinnamon Butter

1. Preheat waffle iron. For Cinnamon Butter, combine butter, powdered sugar, orange peel, cinnamon and vanilla in small bowl; mix well. Set aside.

2. Combine muffin mix, buttermilk and egg in medium bowl; stir until just blended.

3. Spray waffle iron with cooking spray. Spoon ½ of batter (1 cup) onto waffle iron and cook according to manufacturer's directions. Repeat with remaining batter. Serve with Cinnamon Butter.   *Makes 4 servings*

½ cup unsalted whipped butter, softened
2 tablespoons powdered sugar
2 teaspoons grated orange peel
¼ teaspoon ground cinnamon
¼ teaspoon vanilla
1 package (7 ounces) banana muffin mix
⅔ cup buttermilk
1 egg

Sunny Day Breakfast Burrito

1 tablespoon butter
½ cup red or green bell
   pepper, chopped
2 green onions, sliced
6 eggs
2 tablespoons milk
¼ teaspoon salt
4 (7-inch) flour tortillas,
   warmed
½ cup shredded colby-Jack
   or Mexican blend
   cheese
½ cup salsa

1. Melt butter in medium skillet over medium heat. Add bell pepper and green onions; cook and stir about 3 minutes or until tender.

2. Beat eggs, milk and salt in medium bowl. Add egg mixture to skillet; reduce heat to low. Cook, stirring gently, until eggs are just set. (Eggs should be soft with no liquid remaining.)

3. Spoon egg mixture down center of tortillas; top with cheese. Fold in sides to enclose filling. Serve with salsa.
Makes 4 servings

Rise & Shine

Fudgey Peanut Butter Chip Muffins

1. Heat oven to 350°F. Line muffin cups (2½ inches in diameter) with paper bake cups.

2. Stir together applesauce and oats in small bowl; set aside. Beat butter, granulated sugar, brown sugar, egg and vanilla in large bowl until well blended. Add applesauce mixture; blend well. Stir together flour, cocoa, baking soda and cinnamon, if desired. Add to butter mixture, blending well. Stir in peanut butter chips. Fill muffin cups ¾ full with batter.

3. Bake 22 to 26 minutes or until wooden pick inserted in center comes out almost clean. Cool slightly in pan on wire rack. Sprinkle muffin tops with powdered sugar, if desired. Serve warm.   *Makes 12 to 15 muffins*

Fudgey Chocolate Chip Muffins: Omit Peanut Butter Chips. Add 1 cup HERSHEY'S Semi-Sweet Chocolate Chips.

½ cup applesauce
½ cup quick-cooking rolled oats
¼ cup (½ stick) butter or margarine, softened
½ cup granulated sugar
½ cup packed light brown sugar
1 egg
½ teaspoon vanilla extract
¾ cup all-purpose flour
¼ cup HERSHEY'S Dutch Processed Cocoa or HERSHEY'S Cocoa
½ teaspoon baking soda
¼ teaspoon ground cinnamon (optional)
1 cup REESE'S® Peanut Butter Chips
Powdered sugar (optional)

Rise & Shine

Apple & Raisin Oven Pancake

1 large baking apple, cored
and thinly sliced
⅓ cup golden raisins
2 tablespoons packed
brown sugar
½ teaspoon ground
cinnamon
4 eggs
⅔ cup milk
⅔ cup all-purpose flour
2 tablespoons butter or
margarine, melted
Powdered sugar
(optional)

1. Preheat oven to 350°F. Spray 9-inch pie plate with nonstick cooking spray.

2. Combine apple, raisins, brown sugar and cinnamon in medium bowl. Transfer to prepared pie plate. Bake, uncovered, 10 to 15 minutes or until apple begins to soften. Remove from oven. *Increase oven temperature to 450°F.*

3. Meanwhile, whisk eggs, milk, flour and butter in medium bowl until blended. Pour batter over apple mixture. Bake 15 minutes or until pancake is golden brown. Invert onto serving dish. Sprinkle with powdered sugar, if desired.

Makes 6 servings

Rise & Shine

Cinnamini Buns

1. Preheat oven to 375°F. Generously grease large baking sheet. Combine brown sugar and cinnamon in small bowl; mix well.

2. Unroll dough and separate into two long (12×4-inch) rectangles; firmly press perforations to seal. Brush dough with melted butter; sprinkle with brown sugar mixture. Roll up each rectangle tightly starting from long side; pinch edges to seal. Cut each roll into 12 (1-inch) slices with serrated knife. Place slices, cut sides up, about 1½ inches apart on prepared baking sheet.

3. Bake about 10 minutes or until golden brown. Remove to wire rack. Blend powdered sugar and milk in small bowl until smooth; add additional milk, if necessary, to reach desired consistency. Drizzle glaze over cinnamon buns.

Makes 2 dozen mini cinnamon buns

2 tablespoons packed brown sugar
½ teaspoon ground cinnamon
1 can (8 ounces) refrigerated crescent roll dough
1 tablespoon butter, melted
½ cup powdered sugar
1 tablespoon milk

1 package DUNCAN
    HINES® Chocolate
    Chip Muffin Mix
¾ cup all-purpose flour
1 teaspoon baking powder
1¾ cups milk
2 eggs
5 tablespoons butter or
    margarine, melted
Confectioners' sugar
    (optional)

Chocolate Chip Waffles

1. Preheat and lightly grease waffle iron according to manufacturer's directions.

2. Combine muffin mix, flour and baking powder in large bowl. Add milk, eggs and melted butter. Stir until moistened, about 50 strokes. Pour batter onto center grids of preheated waffle iron. Bake according to manufacturer's directions until golden brown. Remove baked waffle carefully with fork. Repeat with remaining batter.

3. Dust lightly with confectioners' sugar, if desired. Top with fresh fruit, syrup, grated chocolate or whipped cream, if desired.   *Makes 10 to 12 waffles*

Snacking Surprise Muffins

1. Preheat oven to 400°F. Line 12 medium muffin cups with paper liners. Combine flour, blueberries, ½ cup sugar, baking powder, 1 teaspoon cinnamon and salt in medium bowl. Combine buttermilk, egg and butter in small bowl. Add to flour mixture; mix just until moistened.

2. Spoon about 1 tablespoon batter into each muffin cup. Drop scant teaspoonful of preserves into center of batter in each cup; top with remaining batter. Combine remaining 1 tablespoon sugar and ¼ teaspoon cinnamon in small bowl; sprinkle evenly over batter.

3. Bake 18 to 20 minutes or until lightly browned. Remove muffins to wire rack to cool completely.   *Makes 12 servings*

1½ cups all-purpose flour
1 cup fresh or frozen blueberries
½ cup plus 1 tablespoon sugar, divided
2½ teaspoons baking powder
1¼ teaspoons ground cinnamon, divided
¼ teaspoon salt
⅔ cup buttermilk
1 egg, beaten
¼ cup butter or margarine, melted
3 tablespoons peach preserves

Tooty Fruitys

1 package (10 ounces)
　　extra-light flaky
　　biscuits
10 (1½-inch) fruit pieces,
　　such as plum, apple,
　　peach or pear
1 egg white
1 teaspoon water
　　Powdered sugar
　　(optional)

1. Preheat oven to 425°F. Spray baking sheets with nonstick cooking spray.

2. Separate biscuits. Place on lightly floured surface. Roll each biscuit with lightly floured rolling pin or flatten dough with fingers to form 3½-inch circles. Place 1 fruit piece in center of each circle. Bring 3 edges of dough up over fruit; pinch edges together to seal. Place on prepared baking sheets. Beat egg white and water in small bowl; brush over dough.

3. Bake until golden brown, 10 to 15 minutes. Remove to wire rack to cool. Serve warm or at room temperature. Sprinkle with powdered sugar, if desired, just before serving.
Makes 10 servings

Sweet Tooty Fruitys: Prepare dough circles as directed. Gently press both sides of dough circles into granulated or cinnamon-sugar to coat completely. Top with fruit and continue as directed, except do not brush with egg white mixture or sprinkle with powdered sugar.

Rise & Shine

Strawberry Cinnamon French Toast

1. Preheat oven to 450°F. Spray nonstick baking sheet with nonstick cooking spray.

2. Combine egg, milk and vanilla in shallow dish or pie plate. Lightly dip bread slices in egg mixture until completely coated. Place on baking sheet; bake 15 minutes or until golden, turning over halfway through baking time.

3. Meanwhile, combine butter, sugar and cinnamon in small bowl; stir until well blended. Spread mixture evenly over French toast. Top with strawberries.

Makes 4 servings

1 egg
¼ cup milk
½ teaspoon vanilla
4 (1-inch-thick) diagonally cut slices French bread (about 1 ounce each)
1 tablespoon butter
2 teaspoons sugar
¼ teaspoon ground cinnamon
1 cup sliced strawberries

Reese's® Peanut Butter and Milk Chocolate Chip Crescents

½ cup REESE'S® Peanut Butter and Milk Chocolate Chips
2 tablespoons finely chopped nuts
1 can (8 ounces) refrigerated quick crescent dinner rolls
Peanut Butter Chocolate Drizzle (recipe follows) or powdered sugar (optional)

1. Heat oven to 375°F.

2. Stir together chips and nuts in small bowl. Unroll dough to form 8 triangles. Lightly sprinkle 1 heaping tablespoon chip mixture on top of each; gently press into dough. Starting at shortest side of triangle, roll dough to opposite point. Place rolls, point side down, on ungreased cookie sheet; curve into crescent shape.

3. Bake 10 to 12 minutes or until golden brown. Top with Peanut Butter Chocolate Drizzle or sprinkle with powdered sugar, if desired. Serve warm.

Makes 8 crescents

Peanut Butter Chocolate Drizzle: Place ¼ cup REESE'S® Peanut Butter and Milk Chocolate Chips and 1 teaspoon shortening (do *not* use butter, margarine or oil) in small microwave-safe bowl. Microwave at HIGH (100%) 30 seconds; stir. If necessary, microwave at HIGH an additional 15 seconds at a time, stirring after each heating, just until chips are melted when stirred.

Bunny Pancakes with Strawberry Butter

1. For Strawberry Butter, place cream cheese and butter in food processor or blender; process until smooth. Add sugar; process until blended. Add strawberries; process until finely chopped.

2. Preheat electric skillet or griddle to 375°F. Combine baking mix, milk, eggs and yogurt in medium bowl; mix well. Spoon scant ½ cup batter into skillet. With back of spoon, gently spread batter into 4-inch circle. Spoon about 2 tablespoons batter onto top edge of circle for head. Using back of spoon, spread batter from head to form bunny ears as shown in photo.

3. Cook until bubbles on surface begin to pop and top of pancake appears dry; turn pancake over. Cook until done, 1 to 2 minutes. Decorate with fruit and candies as shown in photo. Repeat with remaining batter. Serve warm with Strawberry Butter. *Makes about 12 (8-inch) pancakes*

1 package (3 ounces) cream cheese, softened
½ cup butter, softened
⅓ cup powdered sugar
1½ cups fresh or thawed frozen strawberries
2 cups buttermilk baking mix
1 cup milk
2 eggs
½ cup plain yogurt
Assorted fruit and candies

Snack Time

Maraschino-Lemonade Pops

1 (10-ounce) jar
   maraschino cherries
8 (3-ounce) paper cups
1 (12-ounce) can frozen
   pink lemonade
   concentrate,
   partially thawed
¼ cup water
8 popsicle sticks

1. Drain cherries, reserving juice. Place one whole cherry in each paper cup. Coarsely chop remaining cherries.

2. Add chopped cherries, lemonade concentrate, water and reserved juice to container of blender or food processor; blend until smooth.

3. Fill paper cups with equal amounts of cherry mixture. Freeze several hours or until very slushy. Place popsicle sticks into center of each cup. Freeze 1 hour longer or until firm. To serve, peel off paper cups.   *Makes 8 servings*

Note: Serve immediately after peeling off the paper cups—these pops melt very quickly.

*Favorite recipe from **Cherry Marketing Institute***

1 cup cottage cheese
1 tablespoon reduced-fat mayonnaise
1 tablespoon lemon juice
2 teaspoons dry ranch-style salad dressing mix
1 can (3 ounces) chunk white tuna packed in water, drained and flaked
2 tablespoons sliced green onion or chopped celery
1 teaspoon dried parsley flakes
1 package (12 ounces) peeled baby carrots

Swimming Tuna Dip

1. Combine cottage cheese, mayonnaise, lemon juice and salad dressing mix in food processor or blender; process until smooth.

2. Combine tuna, green onion and parsley in small bowl. Stir in cottage cheese mixture.

3. Serve dip with carrots.

Makes 4 servings

Pizza Turnovers

1. Preheat oven to 425°F. Spray baking sheet with olive oil cooking spray. Cook sausage in nonstick skillet until browned, stirring to break up meat. Drain off fat. Add pizza sauce; cook and stir until hot.

2. Unroll pizza dough and pat into 12×8-inch rectangle. Cut into 6 (4×4-inch) squares. Divide sausage mixture evenly among squares. Sprinkle with cheese. Lift one corner of each square and fold over filling to opposite corner to form triangle. Press edges with tines of fork to seal. Transfer to prepared baking sheet.

3. Bake 11 to 13 minutes or until golden brown. Serve immediately or follow directions for freezing and reheating. *Makes 6 servings*

Note: To freeze turnovers, remove to wire rack to cool 30 minutes. Individually wrap in plastic wrap; place in freezer container or plastic freezer bag and freeze. To reheat turnovers, preheat oven to 400°F. Unwrap and place on ungreased baking sheet. Cover loosely with foil; bake 18 to 22 minutes or until hot. Or, place one turnover on a paper-towel-lined microwavable plate. Heat on LOW (30% power) 3 to 3½ minutes or until hot, turning once.

6 ounces mild Italian turkey sausage (bulk or removed from casing)
½ cup prepared pizza sauce
1 package (13.8 ounces) refrigerated pizza dough
½ cup shredded Italian cheese blend

Quick S'More

1 whole graham cracker
1 large marshmallow
1 teaspoon hot fudge
  topping

1. Break graham cracker in half crosswise. Place one half on small paper plate or microwavable plate; top with marshmallow.

2. Spread remaining half of cracker with hot fudge topping.

3. Place cracker with marshmallow in microwave. Microwave at HIGH 12 to 14 seconds or until marshmallow puffs up. Immediately place remaining cracker, fudge side down, over marshmallow. Press crackers gently to even out marshmallow layer. Cool completely.   *Makes 1 serving*

Tip: S'mores can be made the night before and wrapped in plastic wrap or sealed in a small plastic food storage bag. Store at room temperature until ready to pack in your child's lunch box the next morning.

Cranberry Gorp

1. Preheat oven to 300°F. Grease 15×10-inch jelly-roll pan. Combine butter, brown sugar and maple syrup in large saucepan; heat over medium heat until butter is melted.

2. Stir in curry powder and cinnamon. Add cranberries, walnuts and pretzels; toss to coat.

3. Spread mixture on prepared pan. Bake 15 minutes or until mixture is crunchy and light brown.   *Makes 20 servings*

¼ cup unsalted butter
¼ cup packed light brown
   sugar
1 tablespoon maple syrup
1 teaspoon curry powder
½ teaspoon ground
   cinnamon
1½ cups dried cranberries
1½ cups coarsely chopped
   walnuts and/or
   slivered almonds
1½ cups lightly salted
   pretzel nuggets

3 cups vanilla frozen yogurt

1 cup reduced-fat (2%) milk

½ cup thawed frozen grape juice concentrate (undiluted)

1½ teaspoons lemon juice

Purple Cow Jumped Over the Moon

1. Place frozen yogurt, milk, grape juice concentrate and lemon juice in food processor or blender container.

2. Process until smooth.

3. Serve immediately. *Makes 8 (½-cup) servings*

Razzmatazz Shake: Place 1 quart vanilla frozen yogurt, 1 cup vanilla yogurt and ¼ cup chocolate syrup in food processor or blender container; process until smooth. Pour ½ of mixture evenly into 12 glasses; top with ½ can (12 ounces) root beer. Fill glasses equally with remaining yogurt mixture; top with remaining root beer. Makes 12 (⅔-cup) servings.

Sunshine Shake: Place 1 quart vanilla frozen yogurt, 1⅓ cups orange juice, 1 cup fresh or thawed frozen raspberries and 1 teaspoon sugar in food processor or blender container; process until smooth. Pour into 10 glasses; sprinkle with ground nutmeg. Makes 10 (½-cup) servings.

Green Meanies

1. Place apple, stem side up, on cutting board. Cut away 2 halves from sides of apple, leaving 1-inch-thick center slice with stem and core. Discard core slice. Cut each half round into 4 wedges using crinkle cutter. Repeat with remaining apples. Each apple will yield 8 wedges.

2. Spread 2 teaspoons nut butter on wide edge of apple slice. Top with another crinkled edge apple slice, aligning crinkled edges to resemble jaws.

3. Insert almond slivers to create fangs.   *Makes 8 servings*

Tip: For best effect, use a crinkle cutter garnishing tool to create a toothy look.

4 green apples
1 cup nut butter
(cashew, almond or
peanut butter)
Almond slivers

1 tablespoon sugar
¼ teaspoon ground
   cinnamon
1 package (6-count)
   refrigerated
   breadsticks

Sugar-and-Spice Twists

1. Preheat oven to 350°F. Spray baking sheet with nonstick cooking spray.

2. Combine sugar and cinnamon in shallow dish or plate.

3. Divide breadstick dough into 6 pieces. Roll each piece into 12-inch rope. Roll in sugar-cinnamon mixture. Twist into pretzel shape; place on prepared baking sheet. Bake 15 to 18 minutes or until lightly browned. Remove from baking sheet; cool 5 minutes. Serve warm. *Makes 6 servings*

Tip: Use colored sugar sprinkles in place of the sugar in this recipe for a fun 'twist' of color that's perfect for holidays, birthdays or simple everyday celebrations.

Señor Nacho Dip

1. Combine cream cheese and Cheddar cheese in small saucepan; stir over low heat until melted.

2. Stir in salsa and milk; cook until heated through, stirring occasionally.

3. Transfer dip to small serving bowl. Serve with tortilla chips. Garnish with hot peppers and cilantro, if desired. *Makes 4 servings*

Olé Dip: Substitute Monterey Jack cheese or taco cheese for Cheddar cheese.

Spicy Mustard Dip: Omit tortilla chips. Substitute 2 teaspoons spicy brown or honey mustard for salsa. Serve with fresh vegetable dippers or pretzels.

4 ounces cream cheese, cubed
½ cup (2 ounces) shredded Cheddar cheese
¼ cup mild or medium chunky salsa
2 teaspoons milk
4 ounces baked tortilla chips or assorted fresh vegetable dippers

1²⁄₃ cups (10-ounce package) HERSHEY'S Mint Chocolate Chips*

2 cups (12-ounce package) HERSHEY'S Semi-Sweet Chocolate Chips

2 tablespoons shortening (do not use butter, margarine, spread or oil)

60 to 70 round buttery crackers (about half of 1-pound box)

Hershey's Easy Chocolate Cracker Snacks

1. Line several trays or cookie sheets with waxed paper.

2. Place mint chocolate chips, chocolate chips and shortening in large microwave-safe bowl. Microwave at HIGH (100%) 1 minute; stir. Continue heating 30 seconds at a time, stirring after each heating, until chips are melted and mixture is smooth when stirred.

3. Drop crackers into chocolate mixture one at a time. Using tongs, push cracker into chocolate so that it is covered completely. (If chocolate begins to thicken, reheat 10 to 20 seconds in microwave.) Remove from chocolate, tapping lightly on edge of bowl to remove excess chocolate. Place on prepared tray. Refrigerate until chocolate hardens, about 20 minutes. For best results, store tightly covered in refrigerator.   *Makes about 5¹⁄₂ dozen snacks*

*2 cups (11.5-ounce package) HERSHEY'S Milk Chocolate Chips and ¹⁄₄ teaspoon pure peppermint extract can be substituted for mint chocolate chips.

Peanut Butter and Milk Chocolate Cracker Snacks: Use 1²⁄₃ cups (10-ounce package) REESE'S® Peanut Butter Chips, 2 cups (11.5-ounce package) HERSHEY'S Milk Chocolate Chips and 2 tablespoons shortening. Proceed as above.

Chocolate Raspberry Cracker Snacks: Use 1²⁄₃ cups (10-ounce package) HERSHEY'S Raspberry Chips, 2 cups (11.5-ounce package) HERSHEY'S Milk Chocolate Chips and 2 tablespoons shortening. Proceed as above.

Bear Bite Snack Mix

1. Preheat oven to 350°F. Combine sugar, cinnamon and nutmeg in small bowl; mix well.

2. Combine cereal, graham crackers, raisins and dried fruit bits on jelly-roll pan. Generously spray with cooking spray. Sprinkle with half of sugar mixture; mix well. Spray again with cooking spray; sprinkle with remaining sugar mixture.

3. Bake 5 minutes; stir. Bake 5 minutes more; stir. Cool completely in pan on wire rack. Store in airtight container.   *Makes 4 cups snack mix*

2 teaspoons sugar
¾ teaspoon ground cinnamon
¼ teaspoon ground nutmeg
1½ cups sweetened corn or oat cereal squares
1 cup teddy bear-shaped graham crackers
1 cup raisins
½ cup dried fruit bits or chopped mixed dried fruit
Nonstick cooking spray

2 (8-inch) flour tortillas
Nonstick cooking spray
⅓ cup shredded Cheddar
cheese
⅓ cup chopped cooked
chicken or turkey
1 green onion, thinly sliced
2 tablespoons mild, thick
and chunky salsa

Wild Wedges

1. Heat large nonstick skillet over medium heat until hot.

2. Spray one side of one flour tortilla with cooking spray; place, sprayed side down, in skillet. Top with cheese, chicken, green onion and salsa. Place remaining tortilla over mixture; spray with cooking spray.

3. Cook 2 to 3 minutes per side or until golden brown and cheese is melted. Cut into 8 triangles. *Makes 4 servings*

Variation: For bean quesadillas, omit the chicken and spread ⅓ cup canned refried beans over one of the tortillas.

Fantasy Cinnamon Applewiches

1. Toast bread. Cut into desired shapes using large cookie cutters.

2. Combine cream cheese and apple in small bowl; spread over toast.

3. Combine sugar and cinnamon in another small bowl; sprinkle evenly over cream cheese mixture.

Makes 4 servings

Tip: Instead of using cookie cutters, you can create your own fun shapes—use a serrated knife for the best results.

4 slices raisin bread
**⅓ cup reduced-fat cream
   cheese**
**¼ cup finely chopped
   unpeeled apple**
1 teaspoon sugar
**⅛ teaspoon ground
   cinnamon**

Peanut Butter & Jelly Shakes

1½ cups vanilla ice cream
¼ cup milk
2 tablespoons creamy peanut butter
6 peanut butter sandwich cookies, coarsely chopped
¼ cup strawberry jam

1. Place ice cream, milk and peanut butter in blender. Blend at medium speed 1 to 2 minutes or until smooth.

2. Add chopped cookies; blend 10 seconds at low speed. Pour into 2 glasses.

3. Place jam and 1 to 2 teaspoons water in small bowl; stir until smooth. Stir 2 tablespoons preserve mixture into each glass. Serve immediately.

Makes 2 servings

Tip For a change of pace, prepare these shakes using different flavors of preserves.

Bananas & Cheesecake Dipping Sauce

1. Place all ingredients except nutmeg and bananas in blender; blend until smooth.

2. Pour 2 tablespoons sauce into each of 6 small plastic containers; sprinkle with nutmeg, if desired. Cover tightly. Refrigerate until needed or place containers in small cooler with ice.

3. To serve, partially peel banana and dip directly into sauce.

Makes 6 servings

Tropical Coconut Cream Dipping Sauce: Substitute coconut extract for vanilla.

½ cup sour cream
2 ounces cream cheese
2 tablespoons plus
    1 teaspoon milk
2 tablespoons sugar
½ teaspoon vanilla
    Nutmeg (optional)
6 medium bananas,
    unpeeled and cut
    crosswise into halves

1½ cups (12 ounces) canned or thawed frozen peach slices, drained
¾ cup peach nectar
1 tablespoon sugar
¼ to ½ teaspoon coconut extract (optional)

Fruit Freezies

1. Place peaches, nectar, sugar and extract, if desired, in food processor or blender container; process until smooth.

2. Spoon 2 tablespoons fruit mixture into each section of ice cube tray.*

3. Freeze until almost firm. Insert frill pick into center of each cube; freeze until firm.   *Makes 12 servings*

Or, pour ⅓ cup fruit mixture into each of 8 plastic popsicle molds or small paper or plastic cups. Freeze until almost firm. Insert wooden stick into center of each mold; freeze until firm. Makes 8 servings.

Apricot Freezies: Substitute canned apricot halves for peach slices and apricot nectar for peach nectar.

Pineapple Freezies: Substitute crushed pineapple for peach slices and unsweetened pineapple juice for peach nectar.

Mango Freezies: Substitute chopped fresh mango for peach slices and mango nectar for peach nectar. Omit coconut extract.

Honey Crunch Popcorn

1. Preheat oven to 300°F. Spray large nonstick baking sheet with nonstick cooking spray. Combine popcorn and pecans in large bowl.

2. Combine brown sugar and honey in small saucepan. Cook over medium heat just until brown sugar is dissolved and mixture comes to a boil, stirring occasionally. Pour over popcorn mixture; toss lightly to coat evenly. Transfer to prepared baking sheet.

3. Bake 30 minutes, stirring after 15 minutes. Spray large sheet of waxed paper with nonstick cooking spray. Transfer popcorn to prepared waxed paper to cool. Store in airtight containers. *Makes 12 servings*

Variation: Add 1 cup chopped, mixed dried fruit immediately after removing popcorn from oven.

3 quarts (12 cups) hot air-popped popcorn
½ cup chopped pecans
½ cup packed brown sugar
½ cup honey

Easy Nachos

4 (6-inch) flour tortillas
  Nonstick cooking spray
4 ounces lean ground
  turkey
⅔ cup salsa (mild or
  medium)
2 tablespoons sliced green
  onion
½ cup (2 ounces) shredded
  Cheddar cheese

1. Preheat oven to 350°F. Cut each tortilla into 8 wedges; lightly spray one side of wedges with cooking spray. Place on ungreased baking sheet. Bake 5 to 9 minutes or until lightly browned and crisp.

2. Meanwhile, cook ground turkey in small nonstick skillet until browned, stirring with spoon to break up meat. Drain off fat. Stir in salsa; cook until hot.

3. Sprinkle meat mixture over tortilla wedges. Sprinkle with green onion; top with cheese. Return to oven 1 to 2 minutes or until cheese melts.

Makes 4 servings

Tip: In a hurry? Substitute baked corn chips for flour tortillas and cooking spray. Proceed as directed.

Dipped, Drizzled & Decorated Pretzels

1. Place chips in microwavable bowl. (Be sure bowl and utensils are completely dry.) Cover with plastic wrap and turn back one corner to vent. Microwave at HIGH for 1 minute; stir. Return to microwave and continue heating in 30-second intervals until chips are completely melted. Check and stir frequently.

2. Dip half of each pretzel rod into melted chocolate and decorate, if desired. Roll coated end of several pretzels in toppings. Drizzle others with contrasting color and flavor of melted chips. (Drizzle melted chocolate from spoon while rotating pretzel to coat evenly.)

3. Place decorated pretzels on cooling rack; set over baking sheet lined with waxed paper. Let coating harden completely. Do not refrigerate.

Makes about 2 dozen pretzels

1 package chocolate or flavored chips (choose semisweet, bittersweet, milk chocolate, green mint, white chocolate, butterscotch, peanut butter or any combination)
1 bag pretzel rods
Assorted toppings: jimmies, sprinkles, chopped nuts, coconut, toasted coconut, cookie crumbs, colored sugars (optional)

Creamy Strawberry-Orange Pops

1 container (8 ounces)
    strawberry-flavored
    yogurt
¾ cup orange juice
2 teaspoons vanilla
2 cups frozen whole
    strawberries
1 packet sugar substitute
    or equivalent of
    2 teaspoons sugar
6 (7-ounce) paper cups
6 wooden sticks

1. Combine yogurt, orange juice and vanilla in food processor or blender; process until smooth.

2. Add frozen strawberries and sugar substitute; process until smooth. Pour into 6 paper cups, filling each about ¾ full.

3. Place in freezer for 1 hour. Insert wooden stick into center of each cup. Freeze completely. Peel cup off each pop before serving   *Makes 6 pops*

Snack Time

Ham and Cheese Corn Muffins

1. Preheat oven to 400°F. Line 9 (2¾-inch) muffin cups with paper liners.

2. Combine muffin mix, ham and cheese in medium bowl. Beat milk, egg and mustard in small bowl. Stir milk mixture into dry ingredients; mix just until moistened.

3. Fill muffin cups two-thirds full with batter. Bake 18 to 20 minutes or until light golden brown. Remove muffin pan to cooling rack. Let stand 5 minutes. Serve warm.

Makes 9 muffins

Serving Suggestion: Serve with honey-flavored butter (blend equal amounts of honey and softened butter until smooth).

1 package (about 8 ounces) corn muffin mix
½ cup chopped deli ham
½ cup (2 ounces) shredded Swiss cheese
⅓ cup milk
1 egg
1 tablespoon Dijon mustard

Inside-Out Turkey Sandwiches

2 tablespoons cream
cheese

2 tablespoons pasteurized
process cheese spread

2 teaspoons chopped green
onion tops

1 teaspoon prepared
mustard

12 thin round slices turkey
breast or smoked
turkey breast

4 large pretzel rods or
unsalted breadsticks

1. Combine cream cheese, process cheese spread, green onion and mustard in small bowl; mix well.

2. Arrange 3 turkey slices on large sheet of plastic wrap, overlapping slices in center. Spread ¼ of cream cheese mixture evenly onto turkey slices, covering slices completely.

3. Place 1 pretzel at bottom edge of turkey slices; roll up turkey around pretzel. (Be sure to keep all 3 turkey slices together as you roll them around pretzel.) Repeat with remaining ingredients.

Makes 4 servings

Brontosaurus Bites

1. Preheat oven to 350°F. Combine popcorn, graham crackers, cereal, pineapple and fruit bits in large bowl. Transfer to 15×10-inch jelly-roll pan. Spray mixture generously with cooking spray.

2. Combine sugar, cinnamon and nutmeg in small bowl. Sprinkle half of sugar mixture over popcorn mixture; toss lightly to coat. Spray mixture again with additional cooking spray. Sprinkle with remaining sugar mixture; toss to coat.

3. Bake 10 minutes, stirring after 5 minutes. Cool completely in pan on wire rack. Add raisins; mix lightly.   *Makes 12 (³⁄₄-cup) servings*

Gorilla Grub: Substitute plain raisins for the yogurt-covered raisins and ¼ cup grated Parmesan cheese for the sugar, cinnamon and nutmeg.

4 cups air-popped popcorn
2 cups mini dinosaur- or teddy bear-shaped graham crackers
2 cups corn cereal squares
1½ cups dried pineapple wedges
1 package (6 ounces) dried fruit bits
Butter-flavored nonstick cooking spray
1 tablespoon plus 1½ teaspoons sugar
1½ teaspoons ground cinnamon
½ teaspoon ground nutmeg
1 cup yogurt-covered raisins

8 ounces fresh or thawed frozen unsweetened strawberries
4 ounces cream cheese, softened
¼ cup sour cream
1 tablespoon sugar

Berry Good Dip

1. Place strawberries in food processor or blender container; process until smooth.

2. Beat cream cheese in small bowl until smooth. Stir in sour cream, strawberry purée and sugar; cover. Refrigerate until ready to serve.

3. Spoon dip into small serving bowl. Garnish with orange peel, if desired. Serve with assorted fresh fruit dippers or angel food cake cubes.

Makes 6 (¼-cup) servings

Peanut Pitas

1. Spread inside of each pita half with 1 teaspoon peanut butter
2. Spread 1 teaspoon spreadable fruit over peanut butter.
3. Fill pita halves evenly with banana slices. Serve immediately.

Makes 8 servings

Honey Bees: Substitute honey for spreadable fruit.

Jolly Jellies: Substitute any flavor jelly for spreadable fruit and thin apple slices for banana slices.

1 package (8 ounces)
   small pita breads,
   cut crosswise in half
16 teaspoons peanut butter
16 teaspoons strawberry
   spreadable fruit
1 large banana, peeled
   and thinly sliced
   (about 48 slices)

2 ripe medium bananas
4 wooden sticks
**½ cup reduced-fat granola
    cereal without raisins**
**⅓ cup hot fudge topping, at
    room temperature**

Frozen Chocolate-Covered Bananas

1. Line baking sheet or 15×10-inch jelly-roll pan with waxed paper. Peel bananas; cut each in half crosswise. Insert wooden stick into center of cut end of each banana about 1½ inches into banana half. Place on prepared baking sheet; freeze until firm, at least 2 hours.

2. Place granola in large plastic food storage bag; crush slightly using rolling pin or meat mallet. Transfer granola to shallow plate. Place hot fudge topping in shallow dish.

3. Working with 1 banana at a time, place frozen banana in hot fudge topping; turn and spread topping evenly over banana with small rubber spatula. Immediately transfer banana to plate with granola; turn to coat lightly. Return to baking sheet in freezer. Repeat with remaining bananas. Freeze until hot fudge topping is very firm, at least 2 hours. Let stand 5 minutes before serving.

Makes 4 servings

Bread Pudding Snacks

1. Combine milk, egg substitute, sugar, vanilla, salt and nutmeg, if desired, in medium bowl; mix well. Add bread; mix until well moistened. Let stand at room temperature 15 minutes.

2. Preheat oven to 350°F. Line 12 medium-size muffin cups with paper liners. Spoon bread mixture evenly into prepared cups; drizzle evenly with butter.

3. Bake 30 to 35 minutes or until snacks are puffed and golden brown. Remove to wire rack to cool completely. *Makes 12 servings*

Note: Snacks will puff up in the oven and fall slightly upon cooling.

1¼ cups milk
½ cup egg substitute
⅓ cup sugar
1 teaspoon vanilla
⅛ teaspoon salt
⅛ teaspoon ground nutmeg (optional)
4 cups ½-inch cinnamon or cinnamon-raisin bread cubes (about 6 bread slices)
1 tablespoon butter or margarine, melted

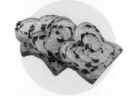

Lunchbox Delights

Funny Face Sandwich Melts

2 super-size English
    muffins, split and
    toasted
8 teaspoons *French's®*
    Sweet & Tangy
    Honey Mustard
1 can (8 ounces) crushed
    pineapple, drained
8 ounces sliced smoked
    ham
4 slices Swiss cheese or
    white American cheese

1. Place English muffins, cut side up, on baking sheet. Spread each with *2 teaspoons* mustard.

2. Arrange one-fourth of the pineapple, ham and cheese on top, dividing evenly.

3. Broil until cheese melts, about 1 minute. Decorate with mustard and assorted vegetables to create your own funny face.   *Makes 4 servings*

Tip: This sandwich is also easy to prepare in the toaster oven.

Prep Time: *10 minutes*
Cook Time: *1 minute*

1 package (3½ ounces)
    soft cheese spread
    with herbs
4 extra-large flour tortillas
1 bag (6 ounces) baby
    spinach
8 ounces thinly sliced
    salami or ham
8 ounces thinly sliced
    Havarti or Swiss
    cheese
1 jar (7 ounces) roasted red
    bell peppers, drained
    and sliced into strips

Backbones

1. Spread 2 to 3 tablespoons cheese close to edge of each tortilla. Layer each tortilla evenly with ¼ of spinach, meat and cheese. Lay thin strips of roasted peppers down center of each tortilla.

2. Tightly roll up tortilla. Slice off and discard rounded ends. Repeat with remaining tortillas and filling.

3. Cut rolls into 1½-inch slices and secure with toothpicks. Two or 3 rolls can be stacked off balance to resemble a backbone.   *Makes 18 servings*

Lunchbox Delights

Tasty Turkey Turnovers

1. Preheat oven to 425°F. Spray baking sheet with nonstick cooking spray.

2. Separate dinner rolls; place on lightly floured surface. With lightly floured rolling pin, roll each piece of dough into 3½-inch circle. Spread honey mustard lightly over dough; top with turkey and broccoli coleslaw. Brush edges of dough with beaten egg white. Fold dough over to form half circle; squeeze edges together firmly with fingers. Press edges with tines of fork to finish sealing.

3. Place on prepared baking sheet; brush egg white over tops of turnovers. Bake about 15 minutes or until golden brown. Let stand 5 minutes before serving. Serve warm or at room temperature with additional mustard for dipping, if desired.

Makes 8 turnovers

1 package (11.3 ounces) refrigerated dinner rolls
2 tablespoons honey mustard
3 ounces thinly sliced deli turkey breast
¾ cup packaged broccoli coleslaw
1 egg white, beaten
Additional mustard (optional)

Hot Dog Burritos

1 can (16 ounces) pork
  and beans
⅓ cup ketchup
2 tablespoons brown sugar
2 tablespoons *French's*®
  Classic Yellow® Mustard
8 frankfurters, cooked
8 (8-inch) flour tortillas,
  heated

1. Combine beans, ketchup, brown sugar and mustard in medium saucepan. Bring to boil over medium-high heat. Reduce heat to low and simmer 2 minutes.

2. Arrange frankfurters in heated tortillas and top with bean mixture.

3. Roll up jelly-roll style.   *Makes 8 servings*

Tip: Try topping dogs with **French's**® French Fried Onions before rolling up!

Prep Time: *5 minutes*
Cook Time: *8 minutes*

Tuna Schooners

1. Combine tuna, apple and carrot in medium bowl. Stir in salad dressing.

2. Spread ¼ of tuna mixture over top of each muffin half.

3. Arrange tortilla chip on each muffin half as shown in photo; press firmly into tuna mixture to form "sail."

Makes 4 servings

2 (3-ounce) cans
  water-packed
  light tuna, drained
½ cup finely chopped apple
¼ cup shredded carrot
⅓ cup reduced-fat ranch
  salad dressing
2 English muffins, split and
  lightly toasted
4 triangular-shaped tortilla
  chips or triangular-
  shaped baked whole
  wheat crackers

1 cup (4 ounces) shredded Cheddar cheese
½ cup finely chopped fresh broccoli
2 tablespoons picante sauce or salsa
4 (6- to 7-inch) corn or flour tortillas
1 teaspoon butter or margarine, divided

Broccoli-Cheese Quesadillas

1. Combine cheese, broccoli and picante sauce in small bowl; mix well.

2. Spoon ¼ of cheese mixture onto 1 side of each tortilla; fold tortilla over filling.

3. Melt ½ teaspoon butter in large nonstick skillet over medium heat. Add 2 quesadillas; cook about 2 minutes on each side or until tortillas are golden brown and cheese is melted. Repeat with remaining butter and quesadillas. Cool completely. *Makes 4 servings*

Tip: Refrigerate individually wrapped quesadillas up to 2 days or freeze up to 3 weeks.

Lunchbox Delights

Grilled Mozzarella & Roasted Red Pepper Sandwich

1. Brush dressing on one side of one bread slice; top with basil, if desired, peppers, cheese and second bread slice.

2. Lightly spray both sides of sandwich with cooking spray.

3. Heat skillet over medium heat until hot. Place sandwich in skillet; cook 4 to 5 minutes on each side or until brown and cheese is melted. Cut into halves.

Makes 1 sandwich

1 tablespoon reduced-fat olive oil vinaigrette or Italian dressing
2 slices (2 ounces) Italian-style sandwich bread
    Fresh basil leaves (optional)
⅓ cup roasted red peppers, rinsed, drained and patted dry
2 slices (1 ounce each) mozzarella or Swiss cheese
    Nonstick olive oil cooking spray

Sub on the Run

2 hard rolls (2 ounces each), split into halves
4 tomato slices
14 turkey pepperoni slices
2 ounces oven-roasted turkey breast
¼ cup (1 ounce) shredded mozzarella or sharp Cheddar cheese
1 cup packaged coleslaw mix or shredded lettuce
¼ medium green bell pepper, thinly sliced (optional)
2 tablespoons prepared Italian salad dressing

1. Top each of two bottom halves of rolls with 2 tomato slices, 7 pepperoni slices, half of turkey, 2 tablespoons cheese, ½ cup coleslaw mix and half of bell pepper slices, if desired.

2. Drizzle with salad dressing. Top with roll tops.

3. Cut into halves, if desired.

Makes 2 servings

Lunchbox Delights

Kids' Wrap

1. Spread 2 teaspoons mustard evenly over one tortilla.

2. Top with 2 cheese halves, half of turkey, half of shredded carrot and half of torn lettuce.

3. Roll up tortilla and cut in half. Repeat with remaining ingredients.

Makes 2 servings

4 teaspoons Dijon honey
    mustard
2 (8-inch) flour tortillas
2 slices American cheese,
    cut in half
4 ounces thinly sliced
    oven-roasted
    turkey breast
½ cup shredded carrot
    (about 1 medium)
3 romaine lettuce leaves,
    washed and torn into
    bite-size pieces

Silly Snake Sandwich

½ cup peanut butter

1 loaf (½ pound) sliced French or Italian bread, about 11 inches long and 3 inches wide

1 *each* red bell pepper, black olive, green olive

½ cup jelly, any flavor

¼ cup marshmallow creme

1. Using small amount of peanut butter, attach first 2 inches (3 to 4 slices) of loaf together to create snake head. Cut bell pepper into 2-inch-long tongue shape. Make very small horizontal cut in heel of bread, being careful not to cut all the way through; insert "tongue" into cut. Cut black olive in half lengthwise; attach to snake head with peanut butter to create eyes. Cut 2 small pieces from green olive; attach with peanut butter to create nostrils. Set snake head aside.

2. Combine remaining peanut butter, jelly and marshmallow creme in small bowl until smooth. Spread on half of bread slices; top with remaining bread slices.

3. Place snake head on large serving tray. Arrange sandwiches in wavy pattern to resemble slithering snake as shown in photo. Serve immediately.

Makes about 8 small sandwiches

Peanut Butter and Jelly Pizza Sandwich

1. Split and toast English muffin. Spread peanut butter on cut sides of English muffin. Spread jam over peanut butter.

2. Top with banana slices. Drizzle with chocolate syrup to taste.

3. Sprinkle with coconut flakes, if desired. Serve warm.   *Makes 1 serving*

1 English muffin
2 tablespoons JIF® Creamy Peanut Butter
2 tablespoons SMUCKER'S® Strawberry Jam
6 to 8 slices banana
Chocolate syrup
Sweetened flaked coconut (optional)

Quick & Easy Meatball Soup

1 package (15 to 18 ounces) frozen Italian sausage meatballs without sauce
2 cans (14 ounces each) Italian-style stewed tomatoes, undrained
2 cans (14 ounces each) beef broth
1 can (14 ounces) mixed vegetables
½ cup uncooked rotini or small macaroni
½ teaspoon dried oregano leaves

1. Thaw meatballs in microwave oven according to package directions.

2. Combine meatballs, tomatoes with juice, broth, vegetables, rotini and oregano in large saucepan. Bring to a boil over high heat.

3. Reduce heat to low; cover and simmer 15 minutes or until pasta is tender.

Makes 4 to 6 servings

Mexican Pita Pile-Ups

1. Combine chicken, tomato, olives, chilies, cilantro, lime juice and cumin in medium bowl. (Mixture can be prepared several hours or up to one day in advance. Cover and refrigerate until ready to use.)

2. Top pita breads evenly with chicken mixture. Sprinkle with cheese.

3. Place pita on microwavable plate. Microwave at HIGH 1 minute or until cheese is melted. Let stand 2 to 3 minutes before serving. Repeat with remaining pitas.

Makes 4 servings

1 cup cooked, diced, boneless skinless chicken breast meat

1 cup chopped seeded tomato

1 can (2¼ ounces) sliced ripe olives, drained

¼ cup chopped mild green chilies

¼ cup chopped fresh cilantro leaves

1 tablespoon lime juice

1 teaspoon ground cumin

4 whole-grain pita bread rounds

1 cup shredded sharp Cheddar cheese

8 assorted round and
   oblong sandwich rolls
Butter
16 to 24 slices assorted cold
   cuts (salami, turkey,
   ham, bologna)
6 to 8 slices assorted
   cheeses (American,
   Swiss, Muenster)
1 firm tomato, sliced
1 cucumber, sliced thinly
Assorted lettuce leaves
Cocktail onions, green
   and black olives,
   cherry tomatoes,
   pickled gherkins,
   radishes, baby corn
   and/or hard-cooked
   eggs

Monster Sandwiches

1. Cut rolls open just below center and spread with butter.

2. Layer meats, cheeses, tomato and cucumber slices and greens to make monster faces. Roll "tongues" from ham slices or make "lips" with tomato slices.

3. Use toothpicks to affix remaining ingredients for eyes, ears, fins, horns and hair. *Makes 8 sandwiches*

Grilled Cheese & Turkey Shapes

1. Spread *1 teaspoon* mustard on each slice of bread. Arrange turkey and cheese on half of the bread slices, dividing evenly. Cover with top halves of bread.

2. Cut out sandwich shapes using choice of cookie cutters. Place cookie cutter on top of sandwich; press down firmly. Remove excess trimmings.

3. Spread butter on both sides of sandwich. Heat large nonstick skillet over medium heat. Cook sandwiches 1 minute per side or until bread is golden and cheese melts. *Makes 4 sandwiches*

Tip: Use 2½-inch star, heart, teddy bear or flower-shaped cookie cutters.

Prep Time: *15 minutes*
Cook Time: *2 minutes*

8 teaspoons *French's®* **Mustard, any flavor**
8 slices seedless rye or sourdough bread
8 slices deli roast turkey
4 slices American cheese
2 tablespoons butter or margarine, softened

Rock 'n' Rollers

4 (6- to 7-inch) flour
    tortillas
4 ounces reduced-fat
    cream cheese, softened
1/3 cup peach preserves
1 cup (4 ounces) shredded
    Cheddar cheese
1/2 cup packed washed fresh
    spinach leaves
3 ounces thinly sliced
    regular or smoked
    turkey breast

1. Spread tortillas evenly with cream cheese; cover with thin layer of preserves. Sprinkle with Cheddar cheese.

2. Arrange spinach leaves and turkey over Cheddar cheese. Roll up tortillas; trim ends. Cover and refrigerate until ready to serve.

3. Cut "rollers" crosswise in half or diagonally into 1-inch pieces.

Makes 4 servings

Sassy Salsa Rollers: Substitute salsa for peach preserves and shredded iceberg lettuce for spinach leaves.

Ham 'n' Apple Rollers: Omit peach preserves and spinach leaves. Substitute lean ham slices for turkey. Spread tortillas with cream cheese as directed; sprinkle with Cheddar cheese. Top each tortilla with about 2 tablespoons finely chopped apple and 2 ham slices; roll up. Continue as directed.

Double-Sauced Chicken Pizza Bagel

1. Place bagel halves on microwavable plate. Spread 1 tablespoon pizza sauce onto each bagel half; top with ¼ cup chicken. Spoon 1 tablespoon pizza sauce over chicken.

2. Sprinkle 2 tablespoons mozzarella cheese over each bagel half. Cover loosely with waxed paper; microwave at HIGH 1 to 1½ minutes or until cheese melts.

3. Carefully remove waxed paper. Sprinkle with 1 tablespoon Parmesan cheese. Let stand 1 minute before serving to cool slightly. (Bagels will be very hot.)

Makes 2 servings

Tip: For crunchier "pizzas," toast bagels before adding toppings.

1 (about 3½ ounces) whole
   bagel, split in half
¼ cup prepared pizza sauce
½ cup diced cooked
   chicken breast
¼ cup (1 ounce) shredded
   mozzarella cheese
2 tablespoon grated
   Parmesan cheese

Tangy Italian Chicken Sandwiches

2 cups (8 ounces) chopped cooked chicken or turkey breast

⅓ cup drained bottled hot or mild pickled vegetables (jardinière)

2 ounces provolone cheese slices, diced

¼ cup chopped fresh parsley

3 tablespoons prepared Italian salad dressing

¼ teaspoon dried oregano leaves

4 pita bread rounds (2 ounces each)

8 leaves romaine or red leaf lettuce

1. Combine chicken, pickled vegetables, cheese, parsley, dressing and oregano in medium bowl; mix well.

2. Cut pitas in half crosswise; gently open. Line each half with lettuce leaf.

3. Divide chicken mixture evenly among pita pockets.   *Makes 4 servings*

Cinnamon-Raisin Roll-Ups

1. Combine cream cheese, carrot, raisins, honey and cinnamon in small bowl; mix well.

2. Spread tortillas evenly with cream cheese mixture, leaving ½-inch border around edge of each tortilla.

3. Place 2 apple wedges down center of each tortilla; roll up. Wrap in plastic wrap; refrigerate until ready to serve. *Makes 4 servings*

Tip: For extra convenience, prepare roll-ups the night before. In the morning, pack a roll-up in your child's lunch box along with a frozen juice box. The juice box will be thawed by lunchtime and will keep the snack cold.

4 ounces cream cheese, softened
½ cup shredded carrot
¼ cup golden or regular raisins
1 tablespoon honey
¼ teaspoon ground cinnamon
4 (7- to 8-inch) whole wheat or regular flour tortillas
8 thin apple wedges (optional)

1 small onion, finely chopped
1 tablespoon *Frank's®*
    RedHot® Original
    Cayenne Pepper Sauce
    or *French's®*
    Worcestershire Sauce
4 frankfurters, chopped
1 can (10½ ounces) kidney
    or black beans, drained
1 can (8 ounces) tomato
    sauce
1 teaspoon chili powder
8 taco shells, heated
    Garnish: chopped
        tomatoes, shredded
        lettuce, sliced olives,
        sour cream, shredded
        cheese
1 cup *French's®* French
    Fried Onions

Zippity Hot Doggity Tacos

1. Heat *1 tablespoon oil* in 12-inch nonstick skillet over medium-high heat. Cook onion 3 minutes or until crisp-tender. Stir in *Frank's RedHot* Sauce, frankfurters, beans, tomato sauce and chili powder. Bring to a boil.

2. Reduce heat to medium-low and cook 5 minutes, stirring occasionally.

3. To serve, spoon chili into taco shells. Garnish as desired and sprinkle with French Fried Onions. Splash on additional *Frank's RedHot* Sauce for extra zip!

Makes 4 servings

Prep Time: *5 minutes*
Cook Time: *8 minutes*

Lunchbox Delights

Super Spread Sandwich Stars

1. For Super Spread, place chopped apple, peanuts, honey, lemon juice and cinnamon in food processor or blender. Pulse several times until ingredients start to blend, occasionally scraping down sides with rubber spatula. Process 1 to 2 minutes until mixture is smooth and spreadable.

2. For Sandwich Stars, use butter knife to spread about 1 tablespoon Super Spread on 2 slices of bread. Stack them together, spread side up. Top with third slice bread.

3. Place cookie cutter on top of sandwich; press down firmly and evenly. Leaving cookie cutter in place, remove excess trimmings with fingers or butter knife. Remove cookie cutter.

Makes 1¼ cups spread (enough for about 10 sandwiches)

Favorite recipe from **Texas Peanut Producers Board**

**1 Red or Golden Delicious
    apple, peeled, cored
    and coarsely chopped**
1 cup roasted peanuts
⅓ cup honey
1 tablespoon lemon juice
**1 teaspoon ground
    cinnamon**
    Sliced sandwich bread

Tuna Melt

1 can (12 ounces) chunk white tuna packed in water, drained and flaked

1½ cups coleslaw mix

3 tablespoons sliced green onions

3 tablespoons reduced-fat mayonnaise

1 tablespoon Dijon mustard

1 teaspoon dried dill weed

4 English muffins, split and lightly toasted

⅓ cup shredded Cheddar cheese

1. Preheat broiler. Combine tuna, coleslaw mix and green onions in medium bowl. Combine mayonnaise, mustard and dill in small bowl. Stir mayonnaise mixture into tuna mixture.

2. Spread tuna mixture onto muffin halves. Place on broiler pan.

3. Broil 4 inches from heat 3 to 4 minutes or until heated through. Sprinkle with cheese. Broil 1 to 2 minutes more or until cheese melts. *Makes 4 servings*

Kids' Quesadillas

1. To prepare 1 quesadilla, arrange 2 slices of cheese on 1 tortilla. Top with one-fourth of the turkey. Spread with *1½ tablespoons* mustard, then top with another tortilla. Prepare 3 more quesadillas with remaining ingredients.

2. Combine butter and paprika. Brush 1 side of tortilla with butter mixture. Preheat 12-inch nonstick skillet over medium-high heat. Place quesadilla in skillet butter side down and cook 2 minutes. Brush with butter mixture and turn over. Cook 1½ minutes or until golden brown. Repeat with remaining three quesadillas.

3. Cut into wedges before serving. *Makes 4 servings*

Prep Time: *5 minutes*
Cook Time: *15 minutes*

8 slices American cheese
8 (10-inch) flour tortillas
½ pound thinly sliced
    deli turkey
6 tablespoons *French's®*
    Sweet & Tangy
    Honey Mustard
2 tablespoons melted
    butter
¼ teaspoon paprika

Pizza Rollers

1 package (13.8 ounces) refrigerated pizza dough
½ cup pizza sauce
18 slices turkey pepperoni
6 sticks mozzarella cheese

1. Preheat oven to 425°F. Coat baking sheet with nonstick cooking spray.

2. Roll out pizza dough on baking sheet to form 12×9-inch rectangle. Cut pizza dough into 6 (4½×4-inch) rectangles. Spread about 1 tablespoon sauce over center third of each rectangle. Top with 3 slices pepperoni and stick of mozzarella cheese. Bring ends of dough together over cheese, pinching to seal. Place seam side down on prepared baking sheet.

3. Bake in center of oven 10 minutes or until golden brown.

Makes 6 servings

Lunchbox Delights

Croque Monsieur

1. Spread one side of each slice of bread with butter; place butter side down on waxed paper. Top 4 slices of bread with 4 slices of cheese.

2. Spread mustard over cheese; top with ham, turkey and remaining cheese. Close sandwiches with remaining bread slices, butter side out.

3. Heat large skillet or griddle over medium heat until hot. Cook sandwiches in batches in skillet or on griddle until golden brown, about 3 minutes per side.

Makes 4 servings

Prep Time: *8 minutes*
Cook Time: *6 minutes*

- **8 slices firm white sandwich bread**
- **2 tablespoons butter, softened**
- **8 slices SARGENTO® Deli Style Sliced Swiss Cheese**
- **2 tablespoons honey mustard**
- **4 slices CURE 81® ham**
- **4 slices cooked turkey breast**

What's for Dinner?

Traditional Spaghetti Sauce

12 ounces spaghetti
1 pound mild Italian
   sausage
½ cup chopped onion
1 can (14.5 ounces)
   CONTADINA® Recipe
   Ready Diced Tomatoes
   with Roasted Garlic,
   undrained
1 cup chicken broth or
   water
1 can (6 ounces)
   CONTADINA Italian
   Paste with Italian
   Seasonings
1 tablespoon chopped
   fresh parsley

1. Cook pasta according to package directions; drain and keep warm.

2. Crumble sausage into large skillet. Cook over medium-high heat, stirring to break up sausage, 4 to 5 minutes or until no longer pink.

3. Add onion; cook 2 to 3 minutes. Drain. Stir in undrained tomatoes, broth, tomato paste and parsley. Bring to a boil. Reduce heat; cook 10 to 15 minutes or until flavors are blended. Serve sauce over pasta. *Makes 4 to 6 servings*

Shredded BBQ Chicken Sandwiches

1 jar (1 pound 10 ounces)
RAGÚ® Old World
Style® Pasta Sauce
3 tablespoons firmly
packed brown sugar
2 tablespoons apple cider
vinegar
1½ tablespoons chili powder
2 teaspoons garlic powder
1½ teaspoons onion powder
4 boneless, skinless
chicken breast halves
(about 1¼ pounds)
6 hamburger buns or
round rolls

1. In 6-quart saucepot, cook Ragú Pasta Sauce, brown sugar, vinegar, chili powder, garlic powder and onion powder over medium heat, stirring occasionally, 5 minutes.

2. Season chicken, if desired, with salt and ground black pepper. Add chicken to sauce. Reduce heat to medium-low and simmer covered, stirring occasionally, 20 minutes or until chicken is thoroughly cooked. Remove saucepot from heat.

3. Remove chicken from sauce. Using two forks, shred chicken. Return shredded chicken to sauce and heat through. To serve, arrange chicken mixture on buns and garnish, if desired, with shredded Cheddar cheese.   *Makes 6 servings*

Prep Time: *5 minutes*
Cook Time: *30 minutes*

What's for Dinner?

Octo-Dogs and Shells

1. Lay 1 hot dog on side with end facing you. Starting 1 inch from one end of hot dog, slice hot dog vertically in half. Roll hot dog ¼ turn. Starting 1 inch from same end, slice in half vertically again, making 4 segments connected at the top. Slice each segment in half vertically, creating total of 8 "legs." Repeat with remaining hot dogs.

2. Place hot dogs in medium saucepan; cover with water. Bring to a boil over medium-high heat. Remove from heat; set aside.

3. Prepare pasta according to package directions, stirring in vegetables during last 3 minutes of cooking time. Drain; return to pan. Stir in Alfredo sauce. Heat over low heat until heated through. Divide pasta mixture between 4 plates. Drain octo-dogs. Arrange one octo-dog on top of pasta mixture on each plate. Draw faces on "heads" of octo-dogs with mustard. Sprinkle crackers over pasta.

Makes 4 servings

4 hot dogs
1½ cups uncooked small shell pasta
1½ cups frozen mixed vegetables
1 cup prepared Alfredo sauce
Prepared yellow mustard in squeeze bottle
Cheese-flavored fish-shaped crackers

1 pound boneless skinless chicken, cut into 1½-inch pieces

¼ cup *French's®* Sweet & Tangy Honey Mustard

2 cups *French's®* French Fried Onions, finely crushed

Golden Chicken Nuggets

1. Preheat oven to 400°F. Toss chicken with mustard in medium bowl.

2. Place French Fried Onions into resealable plastic food storage bag. Toss chicken in onions, a few pieces at a time, pressing gently to adhere.

3. Place nuggets in shallow baking pan. Bake 15 minutes or until chicken is no longer pink in center. Serve with additional honey mustard.

Makes 4 servings

Prep Time: *5 minutes*
Cook Time: *15 minutes*

Monster Mouths

1. Preheat oven to 350°F. Lightly grease 13×9-inch baking dish. Heat oil in large skillet over medium heat. Add onion and bacon; cook until onion is tender. Add beef; cook and stir about 5 minutes or until beef is no longer pink. Stir in tomatoes, salt and black pepper. Stir in cheese. Spoon mixture into cooked shells; place in prepared baking dish.

2. Cut carrots into very thin strips. Cut small slit in olives; poke one end of thin carrot strip into olives for eyes. Cut red bell pepper into fang shapes. Slice pickle lengthwise into tongue shape. Cut cheese slice into zig-zag pattern for teeth.

3. Bake shells 3 to 5 minutes or until hot; remove from oven. Decorate as desired with olive and carrot eyes, bell pepper fangs, pickle tongue and cheese teeth. Serve immediately. *Makes about 6 servings*

1 teaspoon vegetable oil
1 medium onion, chopped
4 slices bacon, chopped
1 pound ground beef
2 medium plum tomatoes, seeded and chopped
½ teaspoon salt
¼ teaspoon black pepper
4 slices American cheese, chopped
½ package (12 ounces) jumbo pasta shells (about 18 shells), cooked and drained
Baby carrots, olives, red bell pepper, small pickles and cheese slices for decoration

What's for Dinner?

1 (6.8-ounce) package
   RICE-A-RONI®
   Spanish Rice
2 tablespoons margarine
   or butter
1 (16-ounce) jar salsa*
12 ounces boneless, skinless
   chicken breasts,
   cut into thin strips
   (about 3 breasts)
1 cup canned black or red
   kidney beans, drained
   and rinsed
1 cup frozen or canned
   corn, drained
8 (6-inch) flour tortillas,
   warmed
   Shredded Cheddar
   cheese and sour cream
   (optional)

Easy Chicken & Rice Wraps

1. In large skillet over medium-high heat, sauté rice-vermicelli mix with margarine until vermicelli is golden brown.

2. Slowly stir in 2 cups water, salsa, chicken and Special Seasonings; bring to a boil. Reduce heat to low. Cover; simmer 15 to 20 minutes or until rice is tender and chicken is no longer pink inside.

3. Stir in beans and corn; let stand 5 minutes before serving. Serve in tortillas with cheese and sour cream, if desired.   *Makes 4 servings*

Or, use 2 cups chopped fresh tomatoes or 1 (14½-ounce) can tomatoes, undrained and chopped, if desired.

Tip: To warm tortillas, wrap them in aluminum foil and bake in a 350°F oven for about 5 minutes. Turn off the heat and keep them in the oven until ready to serve.

Prep Time: 10 minutes
Cook Time: 30 minutes

Mexican Lasagna

1. Preheat oven to 350°F. Set aside 1 cup Ragú Pasta Sauce. In 10-inch skillet, brown ground beef over medium-high heat; drain. Stir in remaining Ragú Pasta Sauce, corn and chili powder.

2. In 13×9-inch baking dish, spread 1 cup sauce mixture. Arrange two tortillas over sauce, overlapping edges slightly. Layer half the sauce mixture and ⅓ of the cheese over tortillas; repeat layers, ending with tortillas. Spread tortillas with reserved sauce.

3. Bake 30 minutes, then top with remaining cheese and bake an additional 10 minutes or until sauce is bubbling and cheese is melted.

Makes 8 servings

Tip: Substitute refried beans for ground beef for a meatless main dish.

Prep Time: *10 minutes*
Cook Time: *40 minutes*

1 jar (1 pound 10 ounces)
RAGÚ® Old World
Style® Pasta Sauce
1 pound ground beef
1 can (15¼ ounces) whole
kernel corn, drained
4½ teaspoons chili powder
6 (8½-inch) flour tortillas
2 cups shredded Cheddar
cheese (about
8 ounces)

Hot Dog Macaroni

1 package (8 ounces)
   hot dogs
1 cup uncooked corkscrew
   pasta
1 cup shredded Cheddar
   cheese
1 box (10 ounces)
   BIRDS EYE® frozen
   Green Peas
1 cup 1% milk

• Slice hot dogs into bite-size pieces; set aside.

• In large saucepan, cook pasta according to package directions; drain and return to saucepan.

• Stir in hot dogs, cheese, peas and milk. Cook over medium heat 10 minutes or until cheese is melted, stirring occasionally.

Makes 4 servings

Prep Time: *10 minutes*
Cook Time: *20 minutes*

What's for Dinner?

Surfin' Salmon

1. Stir together cornflake crumbs, egg substitute, milk, dill weed, pepper and hot pepper sauce in large mixing bowl. Add salmon; mix well.

2. Shape salmon mixture into 5 large egg-shaped balls. Flatten each into ³/₄-inch-thick oval. Pinch one end of each oval into tail shape for fish.

3. Spray large nonstick skillet with cooking spray. Cook fish 2 to 3 minutes over medium-high heat or until lightly browned; turn over. Add oil to skillet; continue cooking 2 to 3 minutes or until firm and lightly browned. Place small drop tartar sauce and pimiento on each fish for "eye." Serve with remaining tartar sauce, if desired. *Makes 5 servings*

Tip: For a tasty side dish of seaplants, serve fish on a bed of shredded Romaine lettuce and matchstick-size cucumber slices.

¹/₃ cup cornflake crumbs
¹/₃ cup egg substitute
2 tablespoons milk
³/₄ teaspoon dried dill weed
¹/₈ teaspoon pepper
   Dash hot pepper sauce
1 (14¹/₂-ounce) can salmon, drained and skin and bones removed
   Nonstick cooking spray
1 teaspoon olive oil
6 tablespoons tartar sauce
5 small pieces pimiento

What's for Dinner?

Mini Mexican Burger Bites

1. Gently combine all ingredients except rolls and cheese in large bowl. Shape into 12 mini patties.

2. Broil or grill patties 4 to 6 minutes for medium doneness (160°F internal temperature), turning once.

3. Arrange burgers on rolls and top with Cheddar cheese. Top with shredded lettuce if desired.

Makes 6 servings

Prep Time: *5 minutes*
Cook Time: *8 minutes*

1½ pounds ground beef
½ cup finely chopped red, yellow or green bell pepper
2 tablespoons *French's®* Worcestershire Sauce
1 teaspoon *Frank's® RedHot®* Original Cayenne Pepper Sauce
1 teaspoon dried oregano leaves
¼ teaspoon salt
12 mini dinner rolls
Shredded Cheddar cheese

What's for Dinner?

Silly Spaghetti Casserole

1. Preheat oven to 350°F. Spray 8-inch square baking dish with nonstick cooking spray. Cook spaghetti according to package directions; drain. Return spaghetti to saucepan. Add Parmesan cheese and egg substitute; mix well. Place in prepared baking dish.

2. Spray large nonstick skillet with cooking spray. Cook turkey and onion in skillet over medium-high heat until meat is lightly browned, stirring to break up meat. Drain fat from skillet. Stir in spinach and pasta sauce. Spoon over spaghetti mixture.

3. Sprinkle with mozzarella cheese. Use small cookie cutter to cut decorative shapes from bell pepper. Arrange on top of cheese. Cover with foil; bake 40 to 45 minutes or until bubbling. Let stand 10 minutes. Cut into squares.

Makes 6 servings

8 ounces uncooked spaghetti, broken in half

¼ cup finely grated Parmesan cheese

¼ cup egg substitute

¾ pound lean ground turkey or ground beef

⅓ cup chopped onion

½ (10-ounce) package frozen cut spinach, thawed and squeezed dry

2 cups pasta sauce

¾ cup (3 ounces) shredded mozzarella cheese

1 red or yellow bell pepper, cored and seeded

Tuna Monte Cristo Sandwiches

4 thin slices (2 ounces)
   Cheddar cheese
4 oval slices sourdough or
   challah (egg) bread
½ pound deli tuna salad
1 egg, beaten
¼ cup milk
2 tablespoons butter or
   margarine

1. Place 1 slice cheese on each bread slice. Spread tuna salad evenly over two slices of cheese-topped bread. Close sandwich with remaining bread.

2. Combine egg and milk in shallow bowl. Dip sandwiches in egg mixture, turning to coat well.

3. Melt butter in large nonstick skillet over medium heat. Add sandwiches; cook 4 to 5 minutes per side or until golden brown and cheese is melted.

Makes 2 servings

Serving suggestion: Serve with a chilled fruit salad.

What's for Dinner?

Mini Chicken Pot Pies

1. Preheat oven to 400°F. Separate biscuits; press into 8 (8-ounce) custard cups, pressing up sides to form crust.

2. Whisk milk and sauce mix in medium saucepan. Bring to boiling over medium-high heat. Reduce heat to medium-low; simmer 1 minute, whisking constantly, until thickened. Stir in chicken and vegetables.

3. Spoon about ⅓ cup chicken mixture into each crust. Place cups on baking sheet. Bake 15 minutes or until golden brown. Top each with cheese and French Fried Onions. Bake 3 minutes or until golden. To serve, remove from cups and transfer to serving plates.   *Makes 8 servings*

Prep Time: *15 minutes*
Cook Time: *about 20 minutes*

- 1 container (about 16 ounces) refrigerated reduced-fat buttermilk biscuits
- 1½ cups milk
- 1 package (1.8 ounces) white sauce mix
- 2 cups cut-up cooked chicken
- 1 cup frozen assorted vegetables, partially thawed
- 2 cups shredded Cheddar cheese
- 2 cups *French's®* French Fried Onions

What's for Dinner?

½ **pound ground beef**
2 cups RAGÚ® Old World
Style® Pasta Sauce
1 can (10¾ to 16 ounces)
baked beans
8 frankfurters, cooked
8 frankfurter rolls

Campfire Hot Dogs

1. In 12-inch skillet, brown ground beef over medium-high heat; drain.

2. Stir in Ragú Pasta Sauce and beans. Bring to a boil over high heat. Reduce heat to low and simmer, stirring occasionally, 5 minutes.

3. To serve, arrange frankfurters in rolls and top with sauce mixture. Garnish, if desired, with Cheddar cheese.   *Makes 8 servings*

Tip: For Chili Campfire Hot Dogs, simply stir 2 to 3 teaspoons chili powder into sauce mixture.

Prep Time: *5 minutes*
Cook Time: *10 minutes*

What's for Dinner?

Ham & Cheese Shells & Trees

1. In large saucepan, bring 2 cups water and margarine to a boil.

2. Stir in pasta. Reduce heat to medium. Gently boil, uncovered, 6 minutes, stirring occasionally. Stir in broccoli; return to a boil. Boil 6 to 8 minutes or until most of water is absorbed.

3. Stir in milk, ham and Special Seasonings. Return to a boil; boil 1 to 2 minutes or until pasta is tender. Let stand 5 minutes before serving.

Makes 4 servings

Tip: No leftovers? Ask the deli to slice a ½-inch-thick piece of ham or turkey.

Prep Time: *5 minutes*
Cook Time: *20 minutes*

2 tablespoons margarine or butter
1 (6.2-ounce) package PASTA RONI® Shells & White Cheddar
2 cups fresh or frozen chopped broccoli
⅔ cup milk
1½ cups ham or cooked turkey, cut into thin strips (about 6 ounces)

What's for Dinner?

Speedy Beef & Bean Burritos

8 (7-inch) flour tortillas
1 pound ground beef
1 cup chopped onion
1 teaspoon minced garlic
1 can (15 ounces) black
    beans, drained and
    rinsed
1 cup spicy thick and
    chunky salsa
2 teaspoons ground cumin
¼ cup cilantro
2 cups (8 ounces) shredded
    cojack or Monterey
    Jack cheese

1. Wrap tortillas in foil; place on center rack in oven. Heat oven to 350°F; heat tortillas 15 minutes.

2. While tortillas are warming, prepare burrito filling. Combine beef, onion and garlic in large skillet; cook over medium-high heat until beef is no longer pink, breaking beef apart with wooden spoon. Pour off drippings.

3. Stir beans, salsa and cumin into beef mixture; reduce heat to medium. Cover and simmer 10 minutes, stirring once. Stir in cilantro. Spoon filling down centers of warm tortillas; top with cheese. Roll up and serve immediately.
.
Makes 4 servings

What's for Dinner?

Zesty Meatball Sandwiches

1. Combine salsa, tomato sauce and chili powder in medium bowl; set aside.

2. Combine beef, egg, bread crumbs, onion, salt and pepper in large bowl; mix well. Form into 16 (about 1½-inch) meatballs.

3. Cook meatballs in large skillet over medium-high heat 6 to 8 minutes or until brown. Add salsa mixture; bring to a boil. Cover; reduce heat to low. Cook, stirring occasionally, 20 to 25 minutes. Place 4 meatballs in each roll; top with salsa mixture. *Makes 4 servings*

1 jar (16 ounces) spicy thick and chunky salsa
1 can (8 ounces) tomato sauce
1 to 2 teaspoons chili powder or chipotle chili powder
1 pound ground beef chuck
1 egg
⅓ cup plain dried bread crumbs
¼ cup minced onion
½ teaspoon salt
½ teaspoon black pepper
4 (6-inch) sourdough or French rolls, split

What's for Dinner?

Twice Baked Potatoes

3 hot baked potatoes,
    split lengthwise
½ cup sour cream
2 tablespoons butter or
    margarine
1⅓ cups *French's®* French
    Fried Onions, divided
1 cup (4 ounces) shredded
    Cheddar cheese,
    divided
Dash paprika (optional)

1. Preheat oven to 400°F. Scoop out inside of potatoes into medium bowl, leaving thin shells.

2. Mash potatoes with sour cream and butter until smooth. Stir in ⅔ *cup* French Fried Onions and ½ cup cheese. Spoon mixture into shells.

3. Bake 20 minutes or until heated through. Top with remaining cheese, onions and paprika, if desired. Bake 2 minutes or until cheese melts.

Makes 6 servings

Tip: To bake potatoes quickly, microwave on HIGH 10 to 12 minutes until tender.

Variation: For added Cheddar flavor, substitute *French's®* **Cheddar French Fried Onions** for the original flavor.

Prep Time: *10 minutes*
Cook Time: *22 minutes*

What's for Dinner?

Taco Pizza

1. Preheat oven to 425°F. Lightly spray 12-inch pizza pan with cooking spray. Unroll pizza dough; press into prepared pan. Build up edges slightly. Prick dough with fork. Bake 7 to 10 minutes or until lightly browned.

2. Meanwhile, lightly spray large nonstick skillet with cooking spray. Add turkey and onion; cook and stir until turkey is no longer pink. Add tomato sauce and taco seasoning to skillet. Bring to a boil. Reduce heat; simmer, uncovered, 2 to 3 minutes. Spoon turkey mixture over warm pizza crust. Bake 5 minutes.

3. Arrange tomatoes over turkey mixture. Sprinkle with cheese. Bake 2 to 3 minutes more or until cheese melts. Top with lettuce. Cut into 8 pieces before serving. *Makes 4 servings*

1 package (13.8 ounces) refrigerated pizza dough
¾ pound ground turkey
½ cup chopped onion
1 can (8 ounces) tomato sauce
1 envelope (1.25 ounces) reduced-sodium taco seasoning
2 medium roma tomatoes, thinly sliced *or* 1 cup chopped tomato
1 cup (4 ounces) shredded Cheddar cheese
1½ cups shredded lettuce

What's for Dinner?

Terrifying Tamale Pie

1 tablespoon vegetable oil
½ cup chopped onion
⅓ cup chopped bell pepper
1 clove garlic, minced
¾ pound ground turkey
¾ teaspoon chili powder
½ teaspoon dried oregano
1 can (14½ ounces)
    Mexican-style stewed
    tomatoes, undrained
1 can (15 ounces) chili
    beans in mild chili
    sauce, undrained
1 cup corn
¼ teaspoon black pepper
1 package (8½ ounces)
    corn muffin mix plus
    ingredients to prepare
    mix
2 cups (8 ounces) taco-
    flavored shredded
    cheese, divided
Assorted vegetables for
    decoration

1. Heat oil in large skillet over medium heat. Add onion and bell pepper; cook until crisp-tender. Stir in garlic. Add turkey; cook until turkey is no longer pink, stirring occasionally. Stir in chili powder and oregano. Add tomatoes with juice; cook and stir 2 minutes, breaking up tomatoes. Stir in beans with sauce, corn and black pepper; simmer 10 minutes or until liquid is reduced by about half.

2. Preheat oven to 375°F. Lightly grease 1½- to 2-quart casserole. Prepare corn muffin mix according to package directions; stir in ½ cup cheese.

3. Spread half of turkey mixture in prepared casserole; sprinkle with ¾ cup cheese. Top with remaining turkey mixture and ¾ cup cheese. Top with corn muffin batter. Decorate with assorted vegetables to make monster face. Bake 20 to 22 minutes or until light golden brown.   *Makes 6 to 8 servings*

Note: Make this pie cute instead of creepy by creating a simple happy face with bell pepper cutouts.

What's for Dinner?

Italian Sloppy Joes

1. Cook sausage with onion and bell pepper in large skillet until no longer pink, stirring often; drain.

2. Add spaghetti sauce and basil; simmer 5 to 7 minutes or until thickened, stirring occasionally.

3. Fill each roll with sausage mixture and slice of cheese.

Makes 4 servings

Prep Time: *8 minutes*
Cook Time: *12 minutes*

1 pound hot or mild bulk Italian sausage (or sausage links with casings removed)
1 small onion, chopped
1 small green or yellow bell pepper, chopped
1 cup prepared spaghetti sauce
1 teaspoon dried basil leaves
4 Kaiser rolls, split, toasted
4 slices SARGENTO® Deli Style Sliced Mozzarella Cheese

What's for Dinner?

Oven-Baked Chicken Parmesan

4 boneless, skinless
   chicken breast halves
   (about 1¼ pounds)
1 egg, lightly beaten
¾ cup Italian seasoned
   dry bread crumbs
1 jar (1 pound 10 ounces)
   RAGÚ® Old World
   Style® Pasta Sauce
1 cup shredded mozzarella
   cheese (about
   4 ounces)

1. Preheat oven to 400°F. Dip chicken in egg, then bread crumbs, coating well.

2. In 13×9-inch glass baking dish, arrange chicken. Bake uncovered 20 minutes.

3. Pour Ragú Pasta Sauce over chicken, then top with cheese. Bake an additional 10 minutes or until chicken is thoroughly cooked. Serve, if desired, with hot cooked pasta.

Makes 4 servings

Prep Time: *10 minutes*
Cook Time: *30 minutes*

What's for Dinner?

Turkey Vegetable Chili Mac

1. Spray large nonstick saucepan or Dutch oven with cooking spray; heat over medium heat until hot. Add turkey, onion and garlic; cook 5 minutes or until turkey is no longer pink, stirring to separate meat.

2. Stir beans, tomatoes with juice, corn and Mexican seasoning into saucepan; bring to a boil over high heat. Cover; reduce heat to low. Simmer 15 minutes, stirring occasionally.

3. Meanwhile, cook pasta according to package directions. Rinse and drain pasta; stir into saucepan. Simmer, uncovered, 2 to 3 minutes or until heated through. Top each serving with dollop of sour cream. Garnish as desired.

Makes 6 servings

¾ pound lean ground turkey
½ cup chopped onion
2 cloves garlic, minced
1 can (about 15 ounces) black beans, rinsed and drained
1 can (14½ ounces) Mexican-style stewed tomatoes, undrained
1 can (14½ ounces) no-salt-added diced tomatoes, undrained
1 cup frozen corn
1 teaspoon Mexican seasoning
½ cup uncooked elbow macaroni
⅓ cup reduced-fat sour cream

What's for Dinner?

1 pound ground beef
1 medium onion, chopped
½ teaspoon salt
1 jar (1 pound 10 ounces)
    RAGÚ® Robusto!™
    Pasta Sauce
1 jar (8 ounces) marinated
    mushrooms, drained
    and chopped
    (optional)
1 cup shredded Cheddar
    cheese (about
    4 ounces)
1 package (2 pounds)
    frozen pizza dough,
    thawed

Cheeseburger Calzones

1. Preheat oven to 375°F. In 12-inch skillet, brown ground beef with onion and salt over medium-high heat; drain. Stir in 1 cup Ragú Pasta Sauce, mushrooms and cheese.

2. On floured board, cut each pound of dough into 4 pieces; press to form 6-inch circles. Spread ½ cup beef mixture on each dough circle; fold over and pinch edges to close.

3. With large spatula, gently arrange calzones on cookie sheets. Bake 25 minutes or until golden. Serve with remaining sauce, heated.

Makes 8 servings

Prep Time: *15 minutes*
Cook Time: *25 minutes*

What's for Dinner?

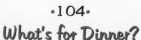

Make Your Own Pizza Shapes

1. Preheat oven to 425°F. Unroll dough onto greased baking sheet. Press or roll dough into 12×8-inch rectangle. With sharp knife or pizza cutter, cut dough into large shape of your choice (butterfly, heart, star). Reroll scraps and cut into mini shapes.

2. Pre-bake crust 7 minutes or until crust just begins to brown. Spread with sauce and top with cheese. Bake 6 minutes or until crust is deep golden brown.

3. Sprinkle with French Fried Onions. Bake 2 minutes longer or until golden.

Makes 4 to 6 servings

Prep Time: *10 minutes*
Cook Time: *15 minutes*

1 package (13.8 ounces) refrigerated pizza dough
¼ to ½ cup prepared pizza sauce
1 cup shredded mozzarella cheese
1 cup *French's*® French Fried Onions

What's for Dinner?

1 tablespoon vegetable oil
½ cup chopped onion
1 can (15 ounces) black
    beans, drained and
    rinsed
1 can (14½ ounces)
    Mexican- or Italian-
    style diced tomatoes,
    undrained
1 cup frozen corn
1 envelope (1¼ ounces)
    taco seasoning mix
6 corn tortillas (6 inches)
2 cups (8 ounces) taco-
    flavored shredded
    Cheddar cheese
1 cup water
    Sour cream (optional)
    Sliced black olives
    (optional)

Mexican Tortilla Stacks

1. Preheat oven to 350°F. Spray 13×9-inch baking dish with nonstick cooking spray. Heat oil in large skillet over medium-high heat until hot. Add onion; cook and stir 3 minutes or until tender. Add beans, tomatoes with juice, corn and taco seasoning mix. Bring to a boil over high heat. Reduce heat to low and simmer 5 minutes.

2. Place 2 tortillas side by side in prepared dish. Top each tortilla with about ½ cup bean mixture. Sprinkle evenly with ⅓ of cheese. Repeat layers twice, creating 2 tortilla stacks each 3 tortillas high. Pour water around sides of tortillas.

3. Cover tightly with foil and bake 30 to 35 minutes or until heated through. Cut into wedges; serve with sour cream and black olives, if desired.

Makes 6 servings

What's for Dinner?

Kid's Choice Meatballs

1. Preheat oven to 425°F. In bowl, gently mix beef, bread crumbs, cheese, Worcestershire and egg. Shape into 1-inch meatballs.

2. Place meatballs on rack in roasting pan. Bake 15 minutes or until cooked through.

3. In large saucepan, combine meatballs and spaghetti sauce. Cook until heated through. Serve over cooked pasta.

Makes 6 to 8 servings (about 48 meatballs)

Quick Meatball Tip: On waxed paper, pat meat mixture into 8×6×1-inch rectangle. With knife, cut crosswise and lengthwise into 1-inch rows. Roll each small square into a ball.

Prep Time: *10 minutes*
Cook Time: *20 minutes*

1½ pounds ground beef
¼ cup dry seasoned bread crumbs
¼ cup grated Parmesan cheese
3 tablespoons *French's*® Worcestershire Sauce
1 egg
2 jars (14 ounces each) spaghetti sauce

What's for Dinner?

Cheddar Cheesesteak Sandwiches

2 tablespoons margarine
or butter
1 large onion, thinly sliced
6 all-beef fresh or frozen
sandwich steaks
1 jar (1 pound) RAGÚ®
Cheese Creations!®
Double Cheddar Sauce
6 hero or sandwich rolls

1. In 12-inch skillet, melt margarine over medium heat and cook onion, covered, stirring occasionally, 4 minutes or until tender. Remove onion and set aside.

2. In same skillet, cook steaks 2 minutes or until done.

3. In 3-quart saucepan, heat Ragú Cheese Creations! Sauce. Arrange steaks and onions in rolls; top with hot sauce.   *Makes 6 servings*

Prep Time: *5 minutes*
Cook Time: *10 minutes*

What's for Dinner?

Hot Diggity Dots & Twisters

1. In large saucepan, bring 1¼ cups water, milk and margarine just to a boil.

2. Stir in pasta, peas and Special Seasonings; return to a boil. Reduce heat to medium. Gently boil uncovered, 7 to 8 minutes or until pasta is tender, stirring occasionally.

3. Stir in hot dogs and mustard. Let stand 3 to 5 minutes before serving.

Makes 4 servings

Prep Time: *5 minutes*
Cook Time: *15 minutes*

⅔ cup milk
2 tablespoons margarine
   or butter
1 (4.8-ounce) package
   PASTA RONI® Four
   Cheese Flavor with
   Corkscrew Pasta
1½ cups frozen peas
4 hot dogs, cut into ½-inch
   pieces
2 teaspoons mustard

What's for Dinner?

Skillet Spaghetti Pizza

1 pound bulk Italian
    sausage
1 tablespoon minced garlic
½ pound uncooked thin
    spaghetti, broken into
    2-inch lengths
1 jar (26 ounces) spaghetti
    sauce
1½ cups water
1 cup (4 ounces) shredded
    mozzarella cheese
½ cup diced green bell
    pepper
1⅓ cups *French's®* French
    Fried Onions

1. Cook sausage and garlic in large nonstick skillet over medium heat until browned, stirring frequently; drain.

2. Stir in uncooked spaghetti, spaghetti sauce and water. Bring to a boil; reduce heat to medium-low. Cover and simmer 15 minutes or until spaghetti is cooked, stirring occasionally.

3. Top spaghetti mixture with cheese, bell pepper and French Fried Onions; remove from heat. Cover and let stand 3 minutes until cheese is melted. Serve immediately.   *Makes 8 servings*

Tip: You may substitute link sausage; remove from casing before cooking.

Variation: Substitute other pizza toppings such as mushrooms, eggplant, olives or pepperoni for green peppers.

Prep Time: *10 minutes*
Cook Time: *23 minutes*

What's for Dinner?

Broiled Turkey Burgers

1. Preheat broiler.

2. Combine turkey, green onions, parsley, ketchup, Italian seasoning, salt and black pepper in large bowl; mix well. Shape turkey mixture into 4 (¾-inch-thick) patties.

3. Spray rack of broiler pan with nonstick cooking spray; place burgers on rack. Broil patties 4 inches from heat 5 to 6 minutes per side or until no longer pink in center. Serve on whole wheat buns with lettuce, grilled pineapple slices and bell pepper strips, if desired.

Makes 4 servings

1 **pound lean ground turkey**
¼ **cup finely chopped green onions**
¼ **cup finely chopped fresh parsley**
1 **tablespoon ketchup**
1 **teaspoon dried Italian seasoning**
¼ **teaspoon salt**
¼ **teaspoon black pepper**
4 **whole wheat hamburger buns**
Toppings: lettuce, grilled pineapple slices and bell pepper strips (optional)

1 jar (28 ounces) pasta
   sauce
6 uncooked lasagna
   noodles
1 container (15 ounces)
   ricotta cheese
2 cups (8 ounces) shredded
   mozzarella cheese or
   pizza cheese blend,
   divided
⅓ cup grated Parmesan
   cheese

No-Fuss Lasagna

1. Preheat oven to 375°F. Spread 1 cup pasta sauce in 11×7-inch baking dish. Arrange 3 uncooked noodles over sauce; top with ricotta cheese, 1 cup mozzarella cheese, Parmesan cheese and 1 cup pasta sauce. Top with remaining 3 uncooked lasagna noodles and remaining pasta sauce.

2. Cover and bake 55 minutes.

3. Uncover and top with remaining 1 cup mozzarella cheese. Bake 5 minutes more or until cheese is melted. Let stand 10 minutes before cutting.

Makes 6 servings

What's for Dinner?

Salsa Macaroni & Cheese

1. In 2-quart saucepan, heat Ragú Cheese Creations! Sauce over medium heat.

2. Stir in salsa; heat through.

3. Toss with hot macaroni. Serve immediately.   *Makes 4 servings*

Prep Time: *5 minutes*
Cook Time: *15 minutes*

1 jar (1 pound) RAGÚ®
  Cheese Creations!®
  Double Cheddar Sauce
1 cup prepared mild salsa
8 ounces elbow macaroni,
  cooked and drained

What's for Dinner?

Sweet Treats

Chocolate Malt Delights

1 package (18 ounces) refrigerated chocolate chip cookie dough
⅓ cup plus 3 tablespoons malted milk powder, original or chocolate flavor, divided
1¼ cups prepared chocolate frosting
1 cup coarsely chopped malted milk balls

1. Preheat oven to 350°F. Grease cookie sheets. Remove dough from wrapper; place in large bowl. Let dough stand at room temperature about 15 minutes.

2. Add ⅓ cup malted milk powder to dough in bowl; beat at medium speed of electric mixer until well blended. Drop rounded tablespoonfuls of dough onto cookie sheet. Bake 10 to 12 minutes or until lightly browned at edges. Cool on cookie sheets 5 minutes; remove to wire racks to cool completely.

5. Combine frosting and remaining 3 tablespoons malted milk powder. Top each cookie with rounded tablespoonful of frosting; garnish with malted milk balls. *Makes about 1½ dozen cookies*

Cookies & Cream Cupcakes

2¼ cups all-purpose flour
1 tablespoon baking powder
½ teaspoon salt
1⅔ cups sugar
1 cup milk
½ cup (1 stick) butter, softened
2 teaspoons vanilla
3 egg whites
1 cup crushed chocolate sandwich cookies (about 10 cookies) plus additional for garnish
1 container (16 ounces) vanilla frosting

1. Preheat oven to 350°F. Lightly grease 24 standard (2½-inch) muffin pan cups or line with paper liners.

2. Sift flour, baking powder and salt together in large bowl. Stir in sugar. Add milk, butter and vanilla; beat with electric mixer at low speed 30 seconds. Beat at medium speed 2 minutes. Add egg whites; beat 2 minutes. Stir in 1 cup crushed cookies.

3. Spoon batter evenly into prepared muffin cups. Bake 20 to 25 minutes or until toothpicks inserted into centers come out clean. Cool in pans on wire racks 10 minutes. Remove to racks; cool completely. Frost cupcakes; garnish with additional crushed cookies.   *Makes 24 cupcakes*

Chocolate Peanut Butter Cookies

1. Preheat oven to 350°F. Grease baking sheets.

2. Combine cake mix, peanut butter, eggs and milk in large mixing bowl. Beat at low speed with electric mixer until blended. Stir in peanut butter pieces.

3. Drop dough by slightly rounded tablespoonfuls onto prepared baking sheets. Bake 7 to 9 minutes or until lightly browned. Cool 2 minutes on baking sheets. Remove to cooling racks. *Makes about 3½ dozen cookies*

Tip: You can use 1 cup peanut butter chips in place of peanut butter pieces.

1 package DUNCAN HINES® Moist Deluxe® Devil's Food Cake Mix
¾ cup crunchy peanut butter
2 eggs
2 tablespoons milk
1 cup candy-coated peanut butter pieces

Hot Fudge Waffle Sundaes

12 frozen mini-waffles
2 tablespoons hot fudge topping
¾ cup Neapolitan ice cream
4 tablespoons aerosol whipped cream
Colored sprinkles (optional)

1. Heat waffles in toaster until lightly browned.

2. Heat hot fudge topping in microwave according to manufacturer's directions.

3. Arrange three waffles on each of four serving plates. Top with 1 tablespoon of each ice cream flavor. Evenly drizzle hot fudge topping over top; garnish with whipped cream and sprinkles, if desired. *Makes 4 servings*

Sweet Treats

Reese's® Peanut Butter and Milk Chocolate Chip Fudge

1. Line 8×8×2-inch baking pan with foil. Butter foil. Set aside.

2. Combine sugar, evaporated milk and butter in heavy medium saucepan. Heat over medium heat, stirring constantly, to a full rolling boil. Boil, stirring constantly, 5 minutes. Remove from heat; stir in marshmallows, chips and vanilla. Stir until marshmallows are melted. Pour into prepared pan. Refrigerate 1 hour or until firm.

3. Cut into shapes with cookie cutters or cut into squares. Store tightly covered in a cool, dry place.   *Makes about 1¾ pounds fudge*

1½ cups sugar
⅔ cup (5-ounce can) evaporated milk
2 tablespoons butter
1½ cups miniature marshmallows
1¾ cups (11-ounce package) REESE'S® Peanut Butter and Milk Chocolate Chips
1 teaspoon vanilla extract

Quick Chocolate Softies

1 package (18¼ ounces) devil's food cake mix
⅓ cup water
¼ cup butter, softened
1 egg
1 cup white chocolate chips
½ cup coarsely chopped walnuts

1. Preheat oven to 350°F. Grease cookie sheets. Combine cake mix, water, butter and egg in large bowl. Beat with electric mixer at low speed until moistened. Increase speed to medium; beat 1 minute. (Dough will be stiff.) Stir in white chocolate chips and nuts; stir until well blended.

2. Drop dough by heaping teaspoonfuls 2 inches apart onto prepared cookie sheets.

3. Bake 10 to 12 minutes or until set. Let cookies stand on cookie sheets 1 minute. Remove cookies to wire racks; cool completely.

Makes about 4 dozen cookies

Chocolate Peanut Butter Cups

1. Preheat oven to 350°F. Place paper liners in 30 (2½-inch) muffin cups.

2. Prepare, bake and cool cupcakes following package directions for basic recipe.

3. Combine Vanilla frosting and peanut butter in medium bowl. Stir until smooth. Frost one cupcake. Decorate with peanut butter cup candy, cut side down. Repeat with remaining cupcakes, frosting and candies.

Makes 30 servings

Tip: You can substitute Duncan Hines® Moist Deluxe® Devil's Food, Dark Chocolate Fudge or Butter Recipe Fudge Cake Mix flavors for Swiss Chocolate Cake Mix.

1 package DUNCAN HINES® Moist Deluxe® Swiss Chocolate Cake Mix
1 container DUNCAN HINES® Creamy Home-Style Classic Vanilla Frosting
½ cup creamy peanut butter
15 miniature peanut butter cup candies, wrappers removed, cut in half vertically

Chocolate Chip-Oat Cookies

1 package (18¼ ounces) yellow cake mix
1 teaspoon baking powder
¾ cup vegetable oil
2 eggs
1 teaspoon vanilla
1 cup uncooked old-fashioned oats
¾ cup semisweet chocolate chips

1. Preheat oven to 350°F. Lightly grease cookie sheets or line with parchment paper.

2. Stir together cake mix and baking powder in large bowl. Add oil, eggs and vanilla; beat by hand until well blended. Stir in oats and chocolate chips.

3. Drop dough by slightly rounded tablespoonfuls, 2 inches apart, onto prepared cookie sheets. Bake 10 minutes or until golden brown. *Do not overbake.* Cool on cookie sheets 5 minutes; remove to wire rack to cool completely.   *Makes 4 dozen cookies*

Sweet Treats

Chocolate Fudge

1. Grease 8-inch square pan. Combine sugar, marshmallow creme, milk, peanut butter and salt in large saucepan. Stir constantly over low heat until blended and mixture comes to a boil.

2. Boil 5 minutes, stirring constantly. Remove from heat. Add chocolate; stir until well blended. Stir in vanilla.

3. Pour into prepared pan; let cool. Cut in candy-sized pieces. Store in covered container. *Makes 1 to 1½ pounds*

Tip: For an even more decadent fudge, stir in ½ cup miniature marshmallows, crushed toffee or chopped nuts with the vanilla.

1½ **cups granulated sugar**
1 **cup marshmallow creme**
½ **cup evaporated milk**
⅓ **cup Reduced Fat JIF®**
   Creamy Peanut Butter
½ **teaspoon salt**
1 **(6-ounce) package**
   semisweet chocolate
   chips
1 **teaspoon vanilla**

Apple, Caramel and Nut Roll-Ups

½ cup chopped pecans
3 large Jonathan apples
1 tablespoon butter or
     margarine
¼ teaspoon ground nutmeg
¼ teaspoon ground
     cinnamon
6 (8-inch) thin flour
     tortillas
¾ cup caramel sauce
     Whipped cream

1. Preheat oven to 300°F. Spread pecans in shallow baking pan. Bake 20 to 30 minutes or until lightly browned; set aside.

2. While toasting pecans, peel, core and slice apples. Place in microwavable container. Top with butter, nutmeg and cinnamon. Microwave, covered, at HIGH 3 minutes or until tender, stirring once. Place tortillas in plastic bag (do not seal). Microwave at HIGH 30 to 45 seconds or until heated through; set aside. Place caramel sauce in microwavable container. Microwave at HIGH 30 to 45 seconds or until hot.

3. Place tortillas flat on work surface. Spoon ⅙ of apples down center of each tortilla. Top with 1 tablespoon nuts and 1 tablespoon sauce. Fold one side of tortilla over filling; roll up. Place on large serving platter or individual plates. Drizzle each roll-up with about 1 tablespoon sauce. Top with whipped cream and nuts.

Makes 6 servings

Sweet Treats

S'More Bars

1. Preheat oven to 350°F. Grease 13×9×2-inch baking pan. Remove dough from wrapper. Press dough into prepared pan. Sprinkle evenly with graham cracker crumbs.

2. Bake 10 to 12 minutes or until edges are golden brown. Sprinkle with marshmallows. Bake 2 to 3 minutes or until marshmallows are puffed. Cool completely on wire rack.

3. Combine chocolate chips and shortening in small resealable plastic food storage bag; seal. Microwave at HIGH (100% power) 1 minute; knead bag lightly. If necessary, microwave at HIGH for additional 30-second intervals until chips and shortening are completely melted and smooth, kneading bag after each 30-second interval. Cut off small corner of bag. Drizzle chocolate over bars. Refrigerate 5 to 10 minutes or until chocolate is set.

Makes 3 dozen bars

1 package (18 ounces) refrigerated chocolate chip cookie dough
¼ cup graham cracker crumbs
3 cups mini marshmallows
½ cup semisweet or milk chocolate chips
2 teaspoons shortening

Reese's® Peanut Butter and Milk Chocolate Chip Clusters

1¾ cups (11-ounce package)
REESE'S® Peanut Butter
and Milk Chocolate
Chips
2 teaspoons shortening
(do not use butter,
margarine, spread
or oil)
2 cups peanuts

1. Place chips and shortening in medium microwave-safe bowl. Microwave at HIGH (100%) 1 minute; stir. If necessary, microwave at HIGH an additional 15 seconds at a time, stirring after each heating, just until chips are melted and mixture is smooth when stirred. Stir in peanuts.

2. Spoon heaping teaspoons of peanut mixture into 1-inch paper candy cups or paper-lined muffin cups.

3. Refrigerate 1 hour or until firm. Store tightly covered in refrigerator.

Makes about 2½ dozen candies

Sweet Treats

Banana & Chocolate Chip Pops

1. Slice banana; place in food processor with yogurt and nutmeg. Process until smooth. Transfer to small bowl; stir in chips.

2. Spoon banana mixture into 4 plastic popsicle molds. Place tops on molds; set in provided stand. Set on level surface in freezer; freeze 2 hours or until firm.

3. To unmold, briefly run warm water over popsicle molds until each pop loosens.

Makes 4 servings

Peanut Butter & Jelly Pops: Stir ¼ cup reduced-fat peanut butter in small bowl until smooth; stir in 1 carton (8 ounces) vanilla yogurt. Drop 2 tablespoons all-fruit strawberry preserves on top of mixture; pull spoon back and forth through mixture several times to swirl slightly. Spoon into 4 molds and freeze as directed above.

Blueberry-Lime Pops: Stir 1 carton (8 ounces) Key lime yogurt in small bowl until smooth; fold in ⅓ cup frozen blueberries. Spoon into 4 molds and freeze as directed above.

1 small ripe banana
1 carton (8 ounces) banana yogurt
⅛ teaspoon ground nutmeg
2 tablespoons mini chocolate chips

Peanut Butter Chips and Jelly Bars

1½ cups all-purpose flour
½ cup sugar
¾ teaspoon baking powder
½ cup (1 stick) cold butter
    or margarine
1 egg, beaten
¾ cup grape jelly
1⅔ cups (10-ounce package)
    REESE'S® Peanut Butter
    Chips, divided

1. Heat oven to 375°F. Grease 9-inch square baking pan.

2. Stir together flour, sugar and baking powder in large bowl. With pastry blender or two knives, cut in butter until mixture resembles coarse crumbs. Add egg; blend well. Reserve 1 cup mixture; press remaining mixture onto bottom of prepared pan. Stir jelly to soften; spread evenly over crust. Sprinkle 1 cup peanut butter chips over jelly. Stir together reserved crumb mixture with remaining ⅔ cup chips; sprinkle over top.

3. Bake 25 to 30 minutes or until lightly browned. Cool completely in pan on wire rack. Cut into bars. *Makes about 16 bars*

Tip: For a whimsical twist on this tried-and-true classic, use cookie cutters to cut out shapes for added fun.

Mini Turtle Cupcakes

1. Heat oven to 350°F. Line 54 mini (1½-inch) muffin cups with paper liners. Prepare brownie batter as directed on package. Stir in chopped pecans.

2. Spoon batter into prepared muffin cups filling ⅔ full. Bake 18 minutes or until toothpicks inserted into centers come out clean. Cool in pans on wire racks 5 minutes. Remove cupcakes to racks; cool completely.

3. Spread frosting over cooled cupcakes; top with toasted pecans. Combine caramels and 1 tablespoon cream in small saucepan. Cook and stir over low heat until caramels are melted and mixture is smooth. Add additional 1 tablespoon cream if needed. Spoon caramel decoratively over cupcakes. Store at room temperature up to 24 hours or cover and refrigerate up to 3 days before serving.

Makes 54 mini cupcakes

1 package (21.5 ounces) brownie mix, plus ingredients to prepare mix
½ cup chopped pecans
1 cup prepared or homemade dark chocolate frosting
½ cup coarsely chopped pecans, toasted
12 caramels
1 to 2 tablespoons whipping cream

Sweet Treats

Happy Ice Cream Mice

2 cups vanilla ice cream
1 package (4 ounces)
  single-serving graham
  cracker crusts
6 chocolate sandwich
  cookies, separated and
  cream filling removed
12 black jelly beans
6 red jelly beans
36 chocolate sprinkles
  (approximately
  ¼ teaspoon)

1. Place 1 rounded scoop (about ⅓ cup) ice cream into each crust. Freeze 10 minutes.

2. Press 1 cookie half into each side of ice cream scoops for ears.

3. Decorate with black jelly beans for eyes, red jelly beans for noses and chocolate sprinkles for whiskers. Freeze 10 minutes before serving.

Makes 6 servings

Peanut Butter Candy Bars

1. Preheat oven to 325°F. Grease 13×9-inch baking pan.

2. Beat sugars, peanut butter and butter in large bowl with electric mixer on medium speed until creamy. Add eggs and vanilla; beat until fluffy. Gradually beat in milk. Gradually add flour and baking powder, beating until well blended. Stir in 1 cup candies and nuts. Spread batter into prepared pan.

3. Bake 40 to 45 minutes or until toothpick inserted in center comes out clean. Cool completely in pan on wire rack. Spread frosting over top of bars. Sprinkle with remaining ⅓ cup candies. Cut into bars.   *Makes 2 dozen bars*

1 cup packed brown sugar
½ cup granulated sugar
¾ cup crunchy peanut butter
½ cup (1 stick) butter, softened
2 eggs
1 teaspoon vanilla
¼ cup milk
1¾ cups all-purpose flour
1 teaspoon baking powder
1 package (10 ounces) candy-coated peanut butter pieces (1⅓ cups), divided
⅓ cup coarsely chopped peanuts
1 container (16 ounces) chocolate frosting

Microwave Chocolate Pudding

¼ cup unsweetened cocoa
   powder
2 tablespoons cornstarch
1½ cups reduced-fat (2%)
   milk
6 to 8 packets sugar
   substitute or equivalent
   of ⅓ cup sugar
1 teaspoon vanilla
⅛ teaspoon ground
   cinnamon
   Assorted small candies
   (optional)

1. Combine cocoa powder and cornstarch in medium microwavable bowl or 1-quart glass measure. Gradually add milk, stirring with wire whisk until well blended.

2. Microwave at HIGH 2 minutes; stir. Microwave at MEDIUM-HIGH (70% power) 3½ to 4½ minutes or until thickened, stirring every 1½ minutes.

3. Stir in sugar substitute, vanilla and cinnamon. Let stand at least 5 minutes before serving, stirring occasionally to prevent skin from forming. Serve warm or chilled. Garnish with candies just before serving, if desired.

Makes 4 (⅓-cup) servings

Sweet Treats

Chocolate Bunny Cookies

1. Preheat oven to 350°F. Grease baking sheets.

2. Combine brownie mix, egg, water and oil in large bowl. Stir with spoon until well blended, about 50 strokes. Drop by level tablespoonfuls 2 inches apart on greased baking sheets. Place two pecan halves, flat-side up, on each cookie for ears. Bake at 350°F for 10 to 12 minutes or until set. Cool 2 minutes on baking sheets. Remove to cooling racks. Cool completely.

3. Spread Dark Chocolate Fudge frosting on one cookie. Place white chocolate chips, upside down, on frosting for eyes and nose. Dot each eye with frosting using toothpick. Repeat for remaining cookies. Allow frosting to set before storing cookies between layers of waxed paper in airtight container.

Makes 4 dozen cookies

Tip: For variety, frost cookies with Duncan Hines® Vanilla Frosting and use semisweet chocolate chips for the eyes and noses.

1 (21-ounce) package DUNCAN HINES® Family-Style Chewy Fudge Brownie Mix
1 egg
¼ cup water
¼ cup vegetable oil
1⅓ cups pecan halves (96)
1 container DUNCAN HINES® Creamy Home-Style Dark Chocolate Fudge Frosting
White chocolate chips

Celebrate!

Cookie Sundae Cups

1 package (18 ounces) refrigerated chocolate chip cookie dough
6 cups ice cream, any flavor
1¼ cups ice cream topping, any flavor
Whipped cream
Colored sprinkles

1. Preheat oven to 350°F. Lightly grease 18 (2½-inch) muffin pan cups. Remove dough from wrapper. Shape dough into 18 balls; press onto bottoms and up sides of prepared muffin cups.

2. Bake 14 to 18 minutes or until golden brown. Cool in muffin cups 10 minutes. Remove to wire rack; cool completely.

3. Place ⅓ cup ice cream in each cookie cup. Drizzle with ice cream topping. Top with whipped cream and colored sprinkles.

Makes 1½ dozen sundae cups

Cake
   1 package DUNCAN
      HINES® Moist Deluxe®
      Devil's Food Cake Mix
   3 eggs
   1⅓ cups milk
   ½ cup vegetable oil

Topping
   1 package (4-serving size)
      banana cream
      instant pudding
      and pie filling mix
   1 cup milk
   1 cup whipping cream,
      whipped
   1 medium banana
      Lemon juice
      Chocolate sprinkles
      for garnish

Chocolate Banana Cake

1. Preheat oven to 350°F. Grease and flour 13×9×2-inch pan.

2. For cake, combine cake mix, eggs, milk and oil in large bowl. Beat at low speed with electric mixer until moistened. Beat at medium speed 2 minutes. Pour into pan. Bake at 350°F for 35 to 38 minutes or until toothpick inserted in center comes out clean. Cool completely.

3. For topping, combine pudding mix and milk in large bowl. Stir until smooth. Fold in whipped cream. Spread on top of cooled cake. Slice banana; dip in lemon juice and arrange on top. Garnish with chocolate sprinkles. Refrigerate until ready to serve. *Makes 12 to 16 servings*

Tip: A wire whisk is a great utensil to use when making instant pudding. It quickly eliminates all lumps.

Cobweb Cups

1. Preheat oven to 350°F. Line 18 standard (2½-inch) muffin pan cups with paper liners. Prepare brownie mix according to package directions for cakelike brownies. Stir in chocolate chips. Spoon batter evenly into prepared muffin pans.

2. Combine cream cheese and egg in small bowl; beat until well combined. Add sugar, flour and vanilla; beat until well combined. Place cream cheese mixture in resealable plastic food storage bag; seal bag. Snip off small corner from one side of bag with scissors. Pipe cream cheese mixture in concentric circle design on each cupcake; draw toothpick through cream cheese mixture, out from center, 6 to 8 times.

3. Bake 20 to 25 minutes or until toothpick inserted into centers comes out clean. Cool in pans on wire racks 15 minutes. Remove to racks; cool completely.

Makes 18 cupcakes

1 package (19.8 ounces) brownie mix, plus ingredients to prepare mix
½ cup mini chocolate chips
2 ounces cream cheese, softened
1 egg
2 tablespoons sugar
2 tablespoons all-purpose flour
¼ teaspoon vanilla

1 package (18¼ ounces)
 yellow cake mix,
 plus ingredients
 to prepare mix
1 container (16 ounces)
 vanilla frosting
1 quart fresh strawberries,
 washed, hulled and
 sliced
1 cup caramel or
 butterscotch ice cream
 topping

Celebrate!

Flapjack Party Stack

1. Preheat oven to 350°F. Grease bottoms and sides of 4 (9-inch) round cake pans; line bottoms with waxed paper. Prepare and bake cake mix according to package directions. Let cakes cool in pans on wire racks 15 minutes. Remove from pans; cool completely.

2. Reserve ¼ cup frosting. Place 1 cake layer on serving plate; spread or pipe ⅓ of remaining frosting in swirls on cake to resemble whipped butter. Top with ¼ of sliced strawberries. Repeat with next 2 cake layers, frosting and strawberries. Top stack with remaining cake layer.

3. Warm caramel topping in microwave just until pourable. Drizzle over cake. Spread or pipe remaining frosting in center; garnish with remaining strawberries.

Makes 12 servings

Kids' Confetti Cake

1. Preheat oven to 350°F. Grease and flour 13×9×2-inch baking pan.

2. For cake, combine cake mix, pudding mix, eggs, water and oil in large bowl. Beat at medium speed with electric mixer 2 minutes. Stir in 1 cup chocolate chips. Pour into prepared pan. Bake at 350°F for 40 to 45 minutes or until toothpick inserted in center comes out clean.

3. For topping, immediately arrange marshmallows evenly over hot cake. Place frosting in microwave-safe bowl. Microwave at HIGH (100% power) 25 to 30 seconds. Stir until smooth. Drizzle evenly over marshmallows and cake. Sprinkle with 2 tablespoons chocolate chips. Cool completely.

Makes 12 to 16 servings

Cake
- 1 package DUNCAN HINES® Moist Deluxe® Classic Yellow Cake Mix
- 1 package (4-serving size) vanilla instant pudding and pie filling mix
- 4 eggs
- 1 cup water
- ½ cup vegetable oil
- 1 cup mini semisweet chocolate chips

Topping
- 1 cup colored miniature marshmallows
- ⅔ cup DUNCAN HINES® Creamy Home-Style Chocolate Frosting
- 2 tablespoons mini chips

Celebrate!

Lazy Daisy Cupcakes

1 package (18¼ ounces)
yellow cake mix,
plus ingredients to
prepare mix
Yellow food coloring
1 container (16 ounces)
vanilla frosting
30 large marshmallows
24 small round candies or
gumdrops

1. Line 24 standard (2½-inch) muffin pan cups with paper liners or spray with nonstick cooking spray. Prepare cake mix and bake in prepared muffin cups according to package directions. Cool in pans on wire racks 15 minutes. Remove cupcakes to wire racks; cool completely.

2. Add food coloring to frosting, a few drops at a time, until desired color is reached. Frost cooled cupcakes with tinted frosting.

3. Cut each marshmallow crosswise into 4 pieces with scissors. Stretch pieces into petal shapes; place 5 pieces on each cupcake to form flower. Place candy in center of each flower. *Makes 24 cupcakes*

Triple Chocolate Brownie Sundae

• Place brownie on bottom of sundae dish.

• Place ice cream on top of brownie.

• Shake HERSHEY'S Chocolate Shell Topping according to instructions. Squeeze generous amount over ice cream. Allow to harden for 30 seconds. Top with REDDI-WIP Whipped Topping.

Makes 1 sundae

1 **brownie**
1 **scoop chocolate ice cream**
   HERSHEY'S Chocolate Shell Topping
   REDDI-WIP® Whipped Topping

Celebrate!

Colorific Pizza Cookie

1 package (17½ ounces) sugar cookie mix

⅔ cup mini candy-coated chocolate pieces

⅓ cup powdered sugar

2 to 3 teaspoons milk

1. Preheat oven to 375°F. Prepare cookie mix according to package directions. Spread into ungreased 12-inch pizza pan. Sprinkle evenly with chocolate pieces; press gently into dough.

2. Bake 20 to 24 minutes or until lightly browned. Cool 2 minutes in pan. Transfer to wire rack and cool completely.

3. Blend powdered sugar and milk until smooth, adding enough milk to reach drizzling consistency. Drizzle icing over cooled pizza cookie with spoon or fork. Cut into wedges.

Makes 12 servings

Celebrate!

Captivating Caterpillar Cupcakes

1. Preheat oven to 350°F. Place paper liners in 24 (2½-inch) muffin cups.

2. Combine cake mix, egg whites, water and oil in large bowl. Beat at low speed with electric mixer until moistened. Beat at medium speed 2 minutes. Fold in ⅓ cup star decors. Fill paper liners about half full. Bake at 350°F for 18 to 23 minutes or until toothpick inserted in center comes out clean. Cool in pans 5 minutes. Remove to cooling racks. Cool completely.

3. Tint Vanilla frosting with green food coloring. Frost one cupcake. Sprinkle ½ teaspoon chocolate cookie crumbs on frosting. Arrange 4 candy-coated chocolate pieces to form caterpillar body. Place jelly bean at one end to form head. Attach remaining star and nonpareil decors with dots of frosting to form eyes. Repeat with remaining cupcakes. *Makes 24 cupcakes*

Tip: To finely crush chocolate sandwich cookies, place cookies in resealable plastic bag. Remove excess air from bag; seal. Press rolling pin on top of cookies to break into pieces. Continue pressing until evenly crushed.

1 package DUNCAN HINES® Moist Deluxe® White Cake Mix
3 egg whites
1⅓ cups water
2 tablespoons vegetable oil
½ cup star decors, divided
1 container DUNCAN HINES® Vanilla Frosting
Green food coloring
6 chocolate sandwich cookies, finely crushed (see Tip)
½ cup candy-coated chocolate pieces
⅓ cup assorted jelly beans
Assorted nonpareil decors

Celebrate!

1 (14-ounce) can EAGLE
  BRAND® Sweetened
  Condensed Milk
  (NOT evaporated
  milk), divided
1½ cups milk chocolate
  chips, divided
1 cup miniature
  marshmallows
11 whole graham crackers,
  halved crosswise
Toppings: chopped
  peanuts, mini candy-
  coated chocolate
  pieces, sprinkles

S'Mores on a Stick

1. Microwave half of Eagle Brand in microwave-safe bowl at HIGH (100% power) 1½ minutes. Stir in 1 cup chips until smooth; stir in marshmallows.

2. Spread chocolate mixture evenly by heaping tablespoonfuls onto 11 graham cracker halves. Top with remaining graham cracker halves; place on waxed paper.

3. Microwave remaining Eagle Brand at HIGH (100% power) 1½ minutes; stir in remaining ½ cup chips, stirring until smooth. Drizzle mixture over cookies and sprinkle with desired toppings. Let stand for 2 hours; insert wooden craft stick into center of each cookie. *Makes 11 servings*

Prep Time: *10 minutes*
Cook Time: *3 minutes*

Celebrate!

Peanut Butter Cup Cookie Ice Cream Pie

1. Place large bowl in freezer. Mix peanut butter and honey in medium bowl. Place ice cream in bowl from freezer; add peanut butter mixture and cookies. Mix on low speed with electric mixer until blended.

2. Spoon half of ice cream mixture into crust. Spread chocolate syrup over ice cream mixture in crust. Spoon remaining ice cream mixture over chocolate syrup.

3. Garnish with whipped cream and additional chocolate syrup. Freeze leftovers.

Makes 8 servings

Prep Time: *15 minutes*

½ cup creamy peanut butter
¼ cup honey
1 quart (2 pints) vanilla ice cream, softened
1 cup KEEBLER® Chips Deluxe™ With Peanut Butter Cups Cookies, chopped
1 (6-ounce) READY CRUST® Chocolate Pie Crust
½ cup chocolate syrup
Whipped cream

1 package (18¼ ounces)
    chocolate cake mix,
    plus ingredients to
    prepare mix
1 container (16 ounces)
    chocolate frosting
1 package (5 ounces)
    chocolate nonpareil
    candies
72 red cinnamon candies
    Chocolate sprinkles
    Black decorating gel

Cubcakes

1. Line 24 standard (2½-inch) muffin pan cups with paper liners or spray with nonstick cooking spray.

2. Prepare cake mix and bake in muffin pans according to package directions. Cool in pans on wire racks 15 minutes. Remove cupcakes to wire racks; cool completely.

3. Frost cooled cupcakes with chocolate frosting. Use nonpareils for ears and muzzle. Add red candies for eyes and nose. Sprinkle with chocolate sprinkles for fur. Use decorating gel to pipe dots on eyes and to create mouth.

Makes 24 cupcakes

Celebrate!

Banana Fudge Layer Cake

1. Preheat oven to 350°F. Grease and flour two 9-inch round cake pans.

2. Combine cake mix, water, eggs and oil in large bowl. Beat at low speed with electric mixer until moistened. Beat at medium speed 2 minutes. Stir in bananas.

3. Pour into prepared pans. Bake at 350°F for 28 to 31 minutes or until toothpick inserted in center comes out clean. Cool in pans 15 minutes. Remove from pans; cool completely. Fill and frost cake with frosting. Garnish as desired.

Makes 12 to 16 servings

1 package DUNCAN HINES® Moist Deluxe® Yellow Cake Mix
1⅓ cups water
3 eggs
⅓ cup vegetable oil
1 cup mashed ripe bananas (about 3 medium)
1 container DUNCAN HINES® Chocolate Frosting

Celebrate!

1 package (18¼ ounces)
    white cake mix,
    plus ingredients to
    prepare mix
2 tablespoons nonpareils*
24 flat-bottomed ice cream
    cones
    Prepared vanilla and
    chocolate frostings
    Additional nonpareils
    and decors

Ice Cream Cone Cupcakes

1. Preheat oven to 350°F. Prepare cake mix according to package directions. Stir in nonpareils.

2. Stand cones in 13×9-inch baking pan or in muffin pan cups. Spoon ¼ cup batter into each ice cream cone.

3. Bake about 20 minutes or until toothpick inserted into centers come out clean. Cool completely on wire racks. Frost cupcakes and decorate as desired.

Makes 24 cupcakes

Nonpareils are tiny, round, brightly colored sprinkles used for cake and cookie decorating.

Note: Cupcakes are best served the day they are prepared. Store loosely covered.

Celebrate!

Cookie Pizza Cake

1. Preheat oven to 350°F. Coat two 12×1-inch round pizza pans with nonstick cooking spray. Press cookie dough evenly into one pan. Bake 15 to 20 minutes or until edges are golden brown. Cool 20 minutes in pan on wire rack. Remove from pan; cool completely on wire rack.

2. Prepare cake mix according to package directions. Fill second pan ¼ to ½ full with batter. (Reserve remaining cake batter for another use, such as cupcakes.) Bake 10 to 15 minutes or until toothpick inserted into center comes out clean. Cool 15 minutes on wire rack. Gently remove cake from pan; cool completely. Combine vanilla frosting and peanut butter in small bowl. Gradually stir in milk, 1 tablespoon at a time, until mixture reaches spreadable consistency.

3. Place cookie on serving plate. Spread peanut butter frosting over cookie. Place cake on top of cookie, trimming cookie to match the size of cake, if necessary. Frost top and side of cake with chocolate frosting. Garnish with peanut butter cups, if desired.

Makes 12 to 14 servings

1 package (18 ounces) refrigerated chocolate chip cookie dough
1 package (18¼ ounces) chocolate cake mix, plus ingredients to prepare mix
1 cup prepared vanilla frosting
½ cup peanut butter
1 to 2 tablespoons milk
1 container (16 ounces) chocolate frosting
Chocolate peanut butter cups, chopped (optional)

Celebrate!

Fudge Ribbon Cake

1 (18¼-ounce) package chocolate cake mix, plus ingredients to prepare mix

1 (8-ounce) package cream cheese, softened

2 tablespoons butter or margarine, softened

1 tablespoon cornstarch

1 (14-ounce) can EAGLE BRAND® Sweetened Condensed Milk (NOT evaporated milk)

1 egg

1 teaspoon vanilla extract
Chocolate Glaze (recipe follows)

1. Preheat oven to 350°F. Grease and flour 13×9-inch baking pan. Prepare cake mix as package directs. Pour batter into prepared pan.

2. In small mixing bowl, beat cream cheese, butter and cornstarch until fluffy. Gradually beat in Eagle Brand. Add egg and vanilla; beat until smooth. Spoon evenly over cake batter.

3. Bake 40 minutes or until wooden pick inserted near center comes out clean. Cool. Prepare Chocolate Glaze and drizzle over cake. Store covered in refrigerator.   *Makes 10 to 12 servings*

Chocolate Glaze: In small saucepan over low heat, melt 1 (1-ounce) square unsweetened or semi-sweet chocolate and 1 tablespoon butter or margarine with 2 tablespoons water. Remove from heat. Stir in ¾ cup powdered sugar and ½ teaspoon vanilla extract. Stir until smooth and well blended. Makes about ⅓ cup.

Prep Time: *20 minutes*
Bake Time: *40 minutes*

Celebrate!

Magical Wizard Hats

1. Line 24 standard (2½-inch) muffin pan cups with paper liners or spray with nonstick cooking spray. Prepare cake mix and bake in muffin cups according to package directions. Cool in pans on wire racks 15 minutes. Remove cupcakes from pans; cool completely on wire racks.

2. Frost cupcakes. Place ½ cup remaining frosting in small bowl; tint with yellow food coloring. Tint remaining frosting with purple or black food coloring.

3. Spread sugar cones with dark frosting, covering completely. Place 1 cone upside down on each frosted cupcake. Spoon yellow frosting into small resealable plastic food storage bag. Cut off small corner of bag. Pipe yellow frosting around base of each frosted cone. Decorate as desired.

Makes 24 cupcakes

1 package (18¼ ounces) cake mix (any flavor), plus ingredients to prepare mix
2 containers (16 ounces each) vanilla frosting
Yellow and purple or black food colorings
2 packages (4 ounces each) sugar cones
Orange sugar, decors and black decorating gel

Banana Split Cake

1 package DUNCAN HINES® Moist Deluxe® Banana Supreme Cake Mix

3 eggs

1⅓ cups water

½ cup all-purpose flour

⅓ cup vegetable oil

1 cup mini semisweet chocolate chips

2 to 3 bananas

1 can (16 ounces) chocolate syrup

1 container (8 ounces) frozen whipped topping, thawed

½ cup chopped walnuts

Colored sprinkles

Maraschino cherries with stems, for garnish

1. Preheat oven to 350°F. Grease and flour 13×9×2-inch pan.

2. Combine cake mix, eggs, water, flour and oil in large bowl. Beat at low speed with electric mixer until moistened. Beat at medium speed 2 minutes. Stir in chocolate chips. Pour into prepared pan. Bake at 350°F for 32 to 35 minutes or until toothpick inserted in center comes out clean. Cool completely.

3. Slice bananas. Cut cake into squares; top with banana slices. Drizzle with chocolate syrup. Top with whipped topping, walnuts and sprinkles. Garnish with maraschino cherries. *Makes 12 to 16 servings*

Tip: Dip bananas in diluted lemon juice to prevent darkening.

Celebrate!

Surprise Package Cupcakes

1. Line 24 standard (2½-inch) muffin cups with paper liners or spray with nonstick cooking spray. Prepare and bake cake mix in prepared muffin cups according to package directions. Cool in pans on wire racks 15 minutes. Remove from pans; cool completely on wire racks.

2. If desired, tint frosting with food coloring, adding a few drops at a time until desired color is reached. Spread frosting over cupcakes.

3. Use decorator icing to pipe "ribbons" on fruit squares to resemble wrapped presents. Place 3 candy presents on each cupcake. Decorate with decors and candles, if desired.

Makes 24 cupcakes

1 package (18¼ ounces) chocolate cake mix, plus ingredients to prepare mix
Food coloring (optional)
1 container (16 ounces) vanilla frosting
1 tube (4¼ ounces) white decorator icing
72 chewy fruit squares
Colored decors and birthday candles (optional)

Celebrate!

2 cups plus 1 tablespoon all-purpose flour, divided
¾ cup granulated sugar
¾ cup packed brown sugar
1 tablespoon baking powder
1 teaspoon salt
½ teaspoon baking soda
1¼ cups milk
½ cup shortening
3 eggs
1½ teaspoons vanilla
½ cup mini semisweet chocolate chips
1 container (16 ounces) vanilla frosting
Assorted candies and food colorings

Celebrate!

Play Ball

1. Preheat oven to 350°F. Line 24 standard (2½-inch) muffin pan cups with paper liners.

2. Combine 2 cups flour, sugars, baking powder, salt and baking soda in medium bowl. Beat milk, shortening, eggs and vanilla in large bowl with electric mixer at medium speed until well combined. Add flour mixture; blend well. Beat at high speed 3 minutes, scraping side of bowl frequently. Toss mini chocolate chips with remaining 1 tablespoon flour; stir into batter. Divide evenly among prepared muffin cups.

3. Bake 20 minutes or until toothpick inserted into centers comes out clean. Cool in pan on wire racks 5 minutes. Remove cupcakes to racks; cool completely. Decorate with desired frostings and candies as shown in photo.

Makes 24 cupcakes

Acknowledgments

The publisher would like to thank the companies and organizations listed below for the use of their recipes and photographs in this publication.

Birds Eye® Foods

Cherry Marketing Institute

Del Monte Corporation

Duncan Hines® and Moist Deluxe® are registered trademarks of Pinnacle Foods Corp.

Eagle Brand® Sweetened Condensed Milk

Egg Beaters®

The Golden Grain Company®

Hershey Foods Corporation

Keebler® Company

Nestlé USA

Reckitt Benckiser Inc.

Reddi-wip® is a registered trademark of ConAgra Brands, Inc.

Sargento® Foods Inc.

Crisco is a registered trademark of the J.M. Smucker Company

Texas Peanut Producers Board

Unilever Foods North America

Index

Metric Conversion Chart

VOLUME MEASUREMENTS (dry)

⅛ teaspoon = 0.5 mL
¼ teaspoon = 1 mL
½ teaspoon = 2 mL
¾ teaspoon = 4 mL
1 teaspoon = 5 mL
1 tablespoon = 15 mL
2 tablespoons = 30 mL
¼ cup = 60 mL
⅓ cup = 75 mL
½ cup = 125 mL
⅔ cup = 150 mL
¾ cup = 175 mL
1 cup = 250 mL
2 cups = 1 pint = 500 mL
3 cups = 750 mL
4 cups = 1 quart = 1 L

VOLUME MEASUREMENTS (fluid)

1 fluid ounce (2 tablespoons) = 30 mL
4 fluid ounces (½ cup) = 125 mL
8 fluid ounces (1 cup) = 250 mL
12 fluid ounces (1½ cups) = 375 mL
16 fluid ounces (2 cups) = 500 mL

WEIGHTS (mass)

½ ounce = 15 g
1 ounce = 30 g
3 ounces = 90 g
4 ounces = 120 g
8 ounces = 225 g
10 ounces = 285 g
12 ounces = 360 g
16 ounces = 1 pound = 450 g

DIMENSIONS

$\frac{1}{16}$ inch = 2 mm
⅛ inch = 3 mm
¼ inch = 6 mm
½ inch = 1.5 cm
¾ inch = 2 cm
1 inch = 2.5 cm

OVEN TEMPERATURES

250°F = 120°C
275°F = 140°C
300°F = 150°C
325°F = 160°C
350°F = 180°C
375°F = 190°C
400°F = 200°C
425°F = 220°C
450°F = 230°C

BAKING PAN SIZES

Utensil	Size in Inches/Quarts	Metric Volume	Size in Centimeters
Baking or Cake Pan (square or rectangular)	8×8×2	2 L	20×20×5
	9×9×2	2.5 L	23×23×5
	12×8×2	3 L	30×20×5
	13×9×2	3.5 L	33×23×5
Loaf Pan	8×4×3	1.5 L	20×10×7
	9×5×3	2 L	23×13×7
Round Layer Cake Pan	8×1½	1.2 L	20×4
	9×1½	1.5 L	23×4
Pie Plate	8×1¼	750 mL	20×3
	9×1¼	1 L	23×3
Baking Dish or Casserole	1 quart	1 L	—
	1½ quart	1.5 L	—
	2 quart	2 L	—